Shadow Awakening:
The Dawn of Human Potential

SHADOW AWAKENING

THE DAWN OF HUMAN POTENTIAL

ODYSSEUS ANDRIANOS

Published by Ultimate Vida, LLC.
978-1-7351659-7-4 E-Book
(Kindle)
978-1-7351659-6-7 Paperback (P.O.D.)

I would like to dedicate this book to the betterment of all beings on the planet. To the transcendence and evolution of humanity so we may live our best lives in harmony, bliss, and abundance for all. May this book guide you back to your heart, connect you with your soul, and live the life you have always deserved.

TABLE OF CONTENTS

ACKNOWLEDGMENTS

My appreciation for the following people is beyond any measure, and I am truly grateful for all the support I received while creating this book. I discovered more about myself, how my own mind/heart works, and I feel more empowered than ever to share this wisdom than ever before. The greatest thing about this book is not only having a means of organizing all my years of studies and coaching into a single masterpiece, but it's having a resource to share with people that can help them on their healing journey.

First off, I would like to thank my parents for their continued loving support throughout my entire life. From a young age, my father showed me that all dreams are possible; his determination is one of my greatest inspirations. My mother has always been my rock, helping me stay strong and get through some of my darkest moments in life. I'll never forget how she was there for me in my late 20s after snapping my Achilles tendon. I faced more shadows during this time than ever before in my life. She helped nurse me back to health and learn to walk again. The greatest gift my parents ever gave me was never forcing any religious or political beliefs on me. They allowed me to be a free spirit, which is a big part of what's opened my mind up to limitless quantum possibilities.

My little brother, who I will always consider one of my best friends, has always held a special place in my heart. Growing up together, we conquered demons and dragons and were Jedi knights playing together in our backyard as young boys. Watching him become such a talented and wise young man has always been a great place of motivation for me. Thanks, kid.

Much gratitude goes out to my friend Chris Milholland who I've known since I was a teen. Not only has he been an amazing and loyal friend for many years, but he was also a huge help in editing my book with his background in journalism from San Diego State University. By the way, Go Aztecs! I would also like to thank my buddies Colin Lewis and John Logan Coots. Years ago, we started a study group that was not only an immense inspiration but kept me focused on studying to level up my skill set. Thanks, fellas.

Big shout out and thanks to Green Door Life and their amazing community. Specifically, to Shannon Morse & Lisa Kirby for helping me with the manifestation of this Shadow Awakening book and video course. They were so helpful and generous in supporting me to create the images utilized in this book to share this story with greater depth.

Some of my greatest inspiration over the years has come from the many great authors and philosophers who created the foundation for much of the wisdom I shared in this book. This list is but a fragment of a long line of amazing souls who have guided me on my journey, Alan Watts, Carl Jung, Ken Wilbur, Lao Tzu, Paul Levy, GI Gurdjieff, Carl Buchheit, Dr. Thurman Fleet, Dr. Joe Dispenza, Dr. David Hawkins, Lillian Bridges, and many more. I am eternally grateful for their wisdom and service to humanity. The tools and clarity presented by these individuals have been a driving force in the evolution of mankind. At the end of this book, I created a list of books for you to get more familiar with their work and a few others.

A big shout to Melissa Drake for guiding me through the process of getting my book out. Being a coach for a living, I realized I needed guidance to get to the finish line, and her support has helped me immensely through the process. She reminds me of why you hire a coach for accountability, support, and clarity when you don't have the experience or know what you are doing. Thank you, Melissa.

The greatest gratitude goes out to all of the clients I've coached over the past 20 years. My experience working with them gave me the ability to test out and put into practice much of the wisdom and tools in this book. Their feedback and support are a big part of what made this dream a reality, and I am eternally grateful for every person I have worked with over the years. I have to give a special shout-out to Catherine Falvey, whom I've worked with for 14+ years. I remember when she provided me with the financial support to open my first coaching facility in my early 20s, and that was the catalyst that really kicked off my career as a coach.

Another client shout-out must go to Leslie Murphy. She helped me take my career to the next level by working with me to open my second coaching facility with her company, WBE, here in northern California. She gave me the opportunity to take my teaching of wellness to a wider audience with speeches, coaching, and wellness challenges. I get lit up with gratitude each time we finish a challenge and see how much weight your employees lost. Thank you, Leslie.

Launching a book is no easy task and it's literally been a shadow work journey just to get to this place where I'm finally ready to launch the book. One challenge I had was picking a launch date and this was remedied by the astrological talents of Susie Smith. She tapped into the cosmos to help me choose the perfect day/time to launch this book. Thank you Susie for your support and love through the final stages of putting this book out.

Lastly, I would like to thank all my other friends and family not mentioned here. You are the reason I created this book. I look out into the world, and all I really want to do is hug every one of you and make sure you feel loved. My hope is that you'll read this book and take a few nuggets of wisdom away that could change your entire life. This is why I got into coaching in the first place—to support the people I care about, who showed me who I am, and who inspired me to go deeper into myself, face my own shadows, and love bigger. Much love to all of you. I hope you enjoy my book, and may we all come together to make the world a better place for generations to come.

INTRODUCTION:
The Quest into Darkness

Humanity stands at the precipice of the most expansive, dynamic, and transformative healing to take place since the dawn of time. It's as though we are about to step off the edge of a cliff…We will either learn to fly and awaken our most divine potential or fall into the abyss of a prison created by the illusions and delusions of our own minds. In truth, as humanity evolves through this paradox of darkness and light, each one of us can choose to go through the darkness to discover our light or keep living in a "false light" reality addicted to the illusion of self with an unintegrated shadow. Now is the time to create our own destiny by unleashing our thoughts, actions, and most importantly our ability to FEEL our emotions, so we can become our own greatest healers. THIS ability to feel our emotions is the dawn of human potential.

For far too long, we have buried our emotions, hidden our wounds, and pushed our pain into the shadows of our unconscious minds. When we lack that empathetic awareness, it leaves us starving for a reconnection to our hearts. More people are beginning to wake up to the reality that we must change our way of thinking. This goes beyond just our way of thinking, and into "feeling" our way back into our hearts through a psycho-spiritual connection. This psycho spiritual connection that I speak of is living in harmony with the Universe's natural laws. In order to do this, we must dive back into ourselves by *awakening the shadow*.

For those of you who do not know what *shadow work* is, it's essentially a process for making ourselves more fully integrated and complete humans. Ironically, this is also what the word "heal" actually means…"to make whole." Many people in this world are limping through life with a fragmented psyche because of their past trauma or generational wounds. They're living in a society that is not equipped to support them, guide them, and most importantly, honor them on their healing path.

The current path we tread is materialism - always looking for more stuff, more this, more that, more things…This path denies a connection to our heart, our spirit, our soul. It's almost as though we've been "bought and souled." Humanity is essentially living in spiritual poverty. Many of us have the feeling that something deep within has been lost, and yet we don't know what that thing is. You could even say that we've become unconscious to our unconsciousness, that we're blinded by the illusion of our own ego and tricked into serving the interests of unconscious programming that we didn't create ourselves.

Mental health problems are reaching an all-time high. Fueled by a lack of emotional intelligence or awareness, we seek external "fixes" to manage the effects without ever properly examining the root causes of our emotional pain. Doctors will hand out pills like candy at a Halloween party while completely ignoring deeper causes of dis-ease. What people need more than pills is to take off the mask they've been using to hide from themselves and everyone else, and begin to face their inner demons and deeply embedded emotional pain. No amount of sex, drugs, alcohol, porn, video games, gambling, or running away will "fix" these things. In reality, there is truly nothing to be fixed. It is the transmutation of energy that sets us free from the cage we've created with our unconscious minds.

The world humanity is currently facing is neither "bad" nor "good." In fact, it's precisely where we need it to be in order for humanity to have a deep and profound awakening. The darkness reveals the light and night is always darkest just before the dawn of a new day. As each human turns within to face their own inner darkness, it will elicit a grand awakening for all of humanity. Healing your own shadow actually heals the collective shadow of all of humanity. The challenge is that few people know precisely how to do this inner work - what is sometimes called "The Great Work." This is what this book is all about - providing you the tools, guidance, support, and a means to rescue the human soul from the unconscious forces which bind it and fully integrate the human psyche.

You will start to see a massive shift on all levels throughout your life once you have done the inner work, faced your shadow, and awakened to your divine potential. The transformation can be seen in a multitude of ways, and not only in how you think, talk, walk, and see yourself. It will also profoundly change your ability to love yourself. Instead of locking away all the energy it takes to repress, suppress, and deny your inner wounds, you now get all this energy back. You can finally love yourself completely and unconditionally.

The things that normally trigger an emotional response will turn into clues for you to get curious and find out what's really going on deep within your psyche. The *limiting beliefs* and stories about your past will begin to shift, and the meaning you've created around them will no longer block and sabotage your progress. Instead of thinking, "I'm not good enough," you now look in the mirror and smile as you realize how worthy you are of living the life of your dreams. All of a sudden, you begin attracting precisely what you deserve into your life with far greater ease. By "attracting" I mean that you will become like a powerful magnet, drawing in the people, places, things, money, and experiences that you have always wished for but could never manifest because your nervous system was not attuned to allow it to occur.

Throughout this book, we will continue to explore the concept that everything is energy, and that all energy has a vibrational frequency. At the most fundamental level, we are energy. Our thoughts have measurable frequencies. We might even say that words are like magical spells which we use to create our reality at each moment. As we shift our thinking from low vibrational (dense) thinking to a *quantum* (infinite) level of consciousness, we no longer sabotage ourselves with these low vibrational emotions. Our minds have the ability to create hell out of heaven, or heaven out of hell. Which will you choose?

When someone is sent to prison, they are given a sentence. Word by word, phrase by phrase, and sentence by sentence, we either set ourselves free to enjoy a life of infinite potential, or lock ourselves deeper in a hellish prison within our own minds. This is why learning to recognize where our thoughts, feelings, and emotions are coming from (and how they manifest our reality) is so crucial to awakening the divine within ourselves. Otherwise, we are consistently living our lives like much of society, from this unconscious place, lacking the awareness of how powerful our unconscious beliefs can be, and how they can keep us locked in a reality where we repeat our future based on our painful past.

The shadow parts of ourselves are not "bad," they have just been kept separate and left unseen. It's not our fault that we have these unacknowledged parts of ourselves. In fact, it's nobody's fault. Many people will point the finger at their parents and say it's "their fault." There may be some truth to this on the surface, but our parents may have been completely unconscious of what they were doing when they passed on the childhood wounds they got from their own parents. These unconscious neuroses that run our lives are often generational. Our parents and grandparents did not have the proper tools to deal with these inner emotional energies, because they simply didn't know about any of this.

For so long, we've lacked even a basic understanding of how our nervous system works, how to deal with our emotions, how to process trauma, and even now humanity is only beginning to take our first baby steps when it comes to navigating the inner world of the psyche. There is great beauty in the recognition of our vast human potential and the realization that, even though we are only beginning to learn to walk with our emotions and intuition, soon we'll be running, dancing, and playing with ease. What this means on an energetic level is that we will become less rigid in our beliefs, and more fluid in our capacity to see objectively rather than subjectively in a flow like state of awareness.

As we shift to a *quantum* perspective, we no longer view life through the limiting lens of our traumatic past where we repress our emotional pain and project it onto others. With the tools in this book, you'll not only learn how to shift your energy to a higher frequency, but you'll also know how to deal with other people who are still stuck in the muck of their own unconscious reality, banging their heads against the walls of the prison they've created in their own minds.

The best way to set ourselves free from this prison is to be brutally honest about the parts of ourselves we have been hiding from. Past clients who've done the inner work and the Shadow Awakening program said they felt as though they had been let out of a cage of their own making. After breaking out, they were now walking around in a zoo where they could observe other people who haven't done the work are still unconsciously trapped behind the bars they've placed between themselves and the life they so desperately crave and deserve.

This is not just a normal book that you passively read, but a "workbook" designed to help you to connect with your shadow, integrate it, and awaken to your highest potential as you alchemize the darkness and ignite the light within yourself. There is also a full video course that complements this book to help you fully apply, implement, and journey deeper into yourself on the path to awakening your shadow. Each chapter of the book has questions and review sections at the end for you to complete and integrate what you've learned. You may choose to write directly in this book, but we also recommend that you keep your own private journal for going deeper into anything that comes up for you.

Take this content and use your own journaling or writing to get your emotional energy out of your head and onto the paper. Removing stagnant energy helps you to stay out of your head and creates space for new thoughts and energy to arrive. This book is simple, yet dynamic, and quite comprehensive in its ability to provide guidance on your shadow work journey. The content is designed to immerse you into the depths of your being and show you how to come back to the surface where you can breathe life into a new and improved version of yourself. Whether you're just getting started on the healing path or you've been doing inner work for years, you will definitely find gold nuggets within these pages.

A key point to realize, as you begin this journey into the abyss of who you are, is that your shadow is 80-90% pure GOLD. It's only by sifting through the 10-20% of darkness that we can elicit our deepest awakening. Most of society is operating from an unconscious place because *shadow work* or *inner work* is still considered "taboo." Many of us were trained at a young age to sweep our emotional pain under the rug and ignore our wounds so we can "Get back to work." This type of attitude is typical of a culture that is "unconscious" and addicted to its own suffering. This addiction to a materialistic "service to self," egoic level of consciousness or shall we say unconsciousness is literally killing our hearts. It's no surprise heart disease is the leading killer in society, because we are so disconnected not only from our hearts, but authentically feeling our emotions. A big part of what's burning us out is an addiction to being in "fight or flight" mode, where our adrenal glands are working in overdrive to get more and more done. This constant overdrive causes great harm to the nervous system and keeps us addicted to our own suffering.

When the nervous system is consistently pushed to the max, it begins to "hard wire" the circuitry of the body to become addicted to stress. This can cause chronic damage to our brains, specifically the hippocampus and amygdala. When we have consistently elevated cortisol levels, this creates an increased *allostatic load* on our bodies. This increased allostatic load can cause our bodies to become weaker over time as we lose our ability to maintain homeostasis. The chronic stress placed on our bodies from being in "fight or flight" mode makes it difficult for our bodies to rest and heal.

Stress is a leading cause of many chronic diseases such as high blood pressure, stroke, heart disease, many types of cancer, and even premature aging. This chronic stress may not always be from what's happening in the moment. It's often past trauma, wounds and even generational trauma that are causing us to burn ourselves out. What this does in the short term is leave us feeling stressed out, with less energy, a more difficult time sleeping or calming down, and less connection to our bodies. A lack of connection to our bodies can have detrimental effects on performance on all levels and extends out to affect our relationships with others as well.

Much of our dis-ease can be mitigated through our *awareness*, which we will go over extensively in this book. **The key to change always begins with our awareness**. It's important to *get curious* about what's triggering us to relapse and keep falling back into old ways of being that do not serve our highest purpose in this life. It's also vital that we be honest about what consistent trends in our life keep throwing us into a loop of the same old self-sabotaging behaviors. If we cannot connect with our feelings and observe how emotions affect us, then change will be quite difficult. Being honest is really about reconnecting with our hearts to fully trust ourselves again or maybe for the very first time.

In learning (or relearning) how to trust ourselves, we can begin to adapt to our current circumstances. Often, what leads us astray from our "golden path" or destiny in life is being maladapted to old ways of being or using "outdated maps" to interpret the world based upon our past experiences. These past experiences often dictate our lives from an unconscious level making us live our lives on autopilot rather than consciously creating our experience. Many people actually allow pain and traumas from the past to define who they are because they identify so deeply with their emotional pain, they think it's "who they are." This makes it challenging (or nearly impossible) for the person who is unconsciously reliving these wounds inside their head to be present with what is actually happening in the current moment. They consistently and unconsciously keep reliving their pain and sabotaging themselves. What's worse is they don't even know they are doing it because they identify so much with the stories or maps from their wounded past.

Most of us are unaware of the generational wounds, limiting beliefs, and ways of being that are unconsciously passed down to us through our families. Some people may even feel they are honoring their parents or keeping with tradition by living in a way that keeps them from progressing in their own lives. Others see their life as predetermined, as though some immutable force of nature in their inherited genetics has made the current situation inescapable. Both of these assertions are entirely untrue (demonstrated through the field of *epigenetics*). Epigenetics is the study of how your behaviors and environment can cause changes that affect the way your genes work. This is why the environment we create within the landscape of our own minds is so critical to creating a life we deserve. We have the full capacity to change, and the tools to manifest this change are staring us right in the face. The information and tools presented here will provide the opportunity to unlock your greatest potential, a potential that has been lying dormant within you, just waiting to be activated.

The gold hidden deep within the dark caverns of your own mind is the fact that many of the traumatic experiences and wounds are actually a gift. When released from their prison of darkness, these experiences will provide you with a well of energy. *Neuroplasticity*, the brain's ability to neurologically rewire synapses to form a new expression of who we are, is proof of how powerful our minds can be. Our emotions are a super power! The ability for us to use our hearts to reconnect the bridge between our minds and our bodies is kryptonite to inner pain. Consciously using our emotions, instead of unconsciously allowing our emotions to use us, will set us free. Tapping into the power of our nervous system to rewire it is how this is done.

I'm excited to accompany you on this journey, this odyssey into the shadow realm. Now begins an epic tale, where you will rewrite your story by reconnecting to your heart and healing generations of pain. Keep in mind that everything is energy, and as you heal yourself it heals the vibrational frequency you've inherited from past generations as well. This journey is not for the faint of heart. We commend you for taking the path less traveled, and thank you for embarking on your healing quest. Here's a last bit of wisdom before you get started:

Do not seek answers. Seek bigger and deeper questions. These questions will guide you into who you truly are and what you've always been capable of.

Enjoy your quest into the shadow realm to discover your true self!

"When we live in the past, we are asleep in the present."

— Joe Dispenza

CHAPTER ONE

Section 1: Quantum Thinking

Unleashing Our Potential

We have all heard the saying: *"You are your own worst enemy."* Well, this is never more true than when we are living our lives in an unconscious state of awareness. What I mean by an unconscious state of awareness is that we are essentially asleep at the wheel of our own existence. We are allowing our past to create our future, and we're almost entirely unaware that we're doing it. It's literally like we are sleepwalking through life.

Through introspection and self-examination, we start to see how our own unconscious mind runs our lives from a space that we call "The Shadow." This shadow is the repressed, suppressed, and denied aspects of ourselves lurking deep in our unconscious minds. Because we remain unaware of them, these unacknowledged parts of ourselves often end up ruling our lives, and this is precisely what keeps us stuck repeating the loop of our traumatic past and weaving it into our future. It can almost seem like we become a magnet to attract and re-experience our trauma and wounds over and over again, as if our inner universe has it out for us and we are destined to destroy ourselves. It can feel this way because we are allowing our unconscious beliefs to run our lives.

Creating the life we deserve is much easier than we think. In fact, it becomes crystal clear to me that if we wish to create a new reality for ourselves, the last thing we should be doing is thinking our way out of it. Instead, we should be "feeling our way into it." This may seem counterintuitive to the logical mind, but it is the first step to accessing the quantum field of infinite possibility.

' we delve into the world of alchemy and shadow
; to the capacities of an alchemically activated
'est the life of our dreams from a quantum level
vn as the *alchemical marriage*. It occurs when
of the brain (called the Bicameral mind) are
operate from this level of consciousness,
'n an ordinary way. Our intuitive nature
.eating the capacity to "Quantum Think,"
.ve with greater ease.

.antum Thinking?

Quantum thinking can most easily be explained as a shift in perception from a linear model of reality which can be measured and has limited-potential, to a non-linear model of reality which is immeasurable and has infinite potential. This may not make sense immediately. Keep in mind that, when we are working with the unconscious mind, things become abstract and illogical. We'll do our best to approach this in a way that makes it easier for the rational mind to comprehend.

It ultimately comes down to this: Are you living your life using a limited and linear *3D model of perception* where your past determines your future, or from a limitless *quantum model of perception* where your future has infinite possibilities?

When you move to a quantum model of thinking, you are able to let go of the stories, the limiting beliefs, duality, and the need to judge everything as either *good* or *bad*. These perceptions can only be expressed based upon the limits of your past experiences. New awareness will start to make more sense as we progress through this section of the book, but the truth is that thinking things are either *good* or *bad* does not allow for the infinite possibilities available to you in the future. What you call *good* or *bad* could only be seen that way based upon your past experience, which completely limits your ability to see all future possibilities. This is how trauma and unconscious wounds can hold us back without us even realizing it.

"There is nothing either good or bad, only thinking makes it so."
—Shakespeare

The quantum model of thinking can also be a powerful tool for healing. By shifting our perception of how we see ourselves today, we can shift how we view the stories about our past that may be guiding our lives unconsciously. This is where *shadow work* comes in, but before we get into shadow work, we have to soften up the dense (egoic) walls we've constructed around our

2   *Odysseus Andrianos*

minds over many years before we access the unconscious mind. These walls were originally put in place to protect us, but now they keep us trapped in a very limited linear model of reality.

How does Quantum Thinking Work?

When our minds are constantly and consistently focused on *low vibrational emotions* - like anger, hatred, sadness, anxiety, or even rage we can become *addicted* to the hormonal response created by our bodies. In extreme cases, we can begin to *identify* with these emotions while at the same time repressing them. We continually point the finger at external things as the cause of our emotional state. Often, these external things we think affect us are actually a reflection or symptom of unresolved *Core Conflicts* within ourselves.

Society doesn't generally allow us to open up and be vulnerable. Most of us were never taught how to express our emotions to others appropriately. On an even more basic level, we were never taught how to identify and process our own emotional states properly. So, when we get triggered into a low-vibe emotional state, many of us return to our self-sabotaging behaviors and ways of being that do not serve our higher purpose or aspirations and limit our available responses. These habitual responses make it difficult to accomplish our goals, live a fulfilling life, and love ourselves unconditionally.

In the course of daily life, our subconscious mind weaves our experiences into stories that we tell about ourselves and the world around us. We all have these stories, and they sound like this. *"Every time I try to meet someone new, it ends in disaster. It will be the same this time, too."* In the linear model of thinking, we filter all our new experiences through these stories. When we have a new experience that is even remotely similar to an old one, it triggers that same story to replay itself, limiting our available responses to this new situation. These triggers are less likely to occur when we think from a *quantum* state of mind. The difference with quantum thinking is that we no longer live in an old story. It becomes much harder to fall back into those same old habits that reflect our unresolved issues. Instead of ignoring or masking the pain of past trauma, we gain the confidence to move through it and discover a whole new world of unlimited potential.

This is *Quantum Thinking*…Seeing your infinite and unlimited potential.

Where does Quantum Thinking Make the Biggest Impact?

Another way of looking at linear and quantum thinking is to compare them to different states of energy and vibration. When operating from low-level vibrational emotions, the energy behaves as a particle. When we experience low vibrational emotions, it is a very slow and *dense* experience. Imagine a bunch of balls all densely packed together, like when you feel deep stress or tension in your neck. This is a physical manifestation of *dense* low vibrational emotions within the body. If it is not addressed, this can lead to the development of physical *dis-ease* within the body over time.

The opposite of this is the *wavy* flow-like state of high-level vibrational emotions. Energy from these experiences appear more like waves because they are less dense and have a higher vibrational frequency. This wavy flow-like state is what gives us access to greater potential. With less *density,* we gain more flexibility and access to new insights. We can shed light on our shadow or unconscious and we can see what was not available to us in the denser low-vibrational frequencies of anger, sadness, rage, or lust.

All of this can be measured and applied in day-to-day life. This will be covered in greater detail throughout this book. First, let's briefly explore the story of a Chinese farmer.

The Story of The Chinese Farmer

Once upon a time there was a Chinese farmer...

One day, the farmer's favorite horse ran away.

*The people of the town came to the farmer and said, "Oh no! What **bad** luck!"*

*The farmer just shrugged his shoulders and responded, "**Maybe**."*

The next day, the farmer's favorite horse returned with three wild horses.

*The people of the town came to the farmer and said, "Wow! What **good** luck!"*

*The farmer just shrugged his shoulders and responded, "**Maybe**."*

On the third day, the farmer's son tried to tame one of the wild horses and fell and broke his leg.

*The people of the town came to the farmer and said, "Oh no! What **bad** luck!"*

*The farmer just shrugged his shoulders and responded, "**Maybe**."*

On the fourth day, the military came to take his son to war, but left him because of his leg.

*The people of the town came to the farmer and said, "Wow! What **good** luck!"*

*The farmer just shrugged his shoulders and responded, "**Maybe**."*

The story of the Chinese farmer demonstrates how the townspeople were operating from the *linear, fixed, dense, 3D Newtonian* model of reality which made them label everything as either *good* or *bad*. But the wise farmer was operating from a *flexible, limitless, wavy, quantum* model of reality which allowed him to see past the stories of things being fixed as either *good* or *bad*. How can anything be *good* or *bad* if our understanding changes from one day to the next? Let me repeat, things can only be *good* or *bad* based upon your past experience which is VERY limiting.

Hopefully, this story can help you begin to realize what is possible when you move to a *quantum* way of thinking. Remember, it's okay to still think in 3D. It's not *good* or *bad*. When you move to a quantum model, you won't be limited by your past. As you progress through this book, you will learn to use your intuition as your guide, to discover and access the infinite quantum possibilities available to you.

Quantum Thinking is a Super Power

When you are quantum thinking, you can see things from all angles, sides, and directions. An example of this is the word *Time*. **Time spelled backward is emit.** Time is a measurement of energy *emitted* in space. In fact, we could say time doesn't exist, it's a man-made creation to measure our experience in this life. What really matters is getting your energy right and learning to calm down your nervous system so you can actually heal. When we are addicted to time, it's like being addicted to getting to the destination and not enjoying the journey to get there.

When you quantum think, you are more in tune with the energy flowing through your body and all around you. You may have experienced this when you were laser-focused on something, or so engaged in an activity that you *lost track of time*. In this state, you don't perceive time. You're not aware of time at all because you are living so fully *in the present moment* and your mind has entered the quantum realm.

How can we enter that type of mental space? How can we reach a place where we can truly love ourselves? Where can we find the appreciation and wisdom to love each moment? This all becomes possible once we learn to *see* that we are floating in a *sea* of infinite quantum possibilities.

Let's return to the words, *time* and *emit*. The energy we emit in the form of our emotions can affect how we experience time. Can you remember a time in the past when you burned yourself on something hot? Intense pain can make a few moments feel like hours. Can you remember a time when you were stuck waiting to find out something very important? A few hours can seem like an eternity. These examples provide the logical mind with a glimpse of what it is to be stuck in a low-vibe 3D linear model of thinking.

Now, bring yourself back to another time in your past, when you were with a close friend or loved one. Were there times when hours passed and it seemed like only minutes? Were you ever having so much fun that you lost track of time? Have you ever been so engaged in a conversation that when you looked at the clock you couldn't understand where the time went? In these situations, it can seem like time doesn't exist because you are so *in the moment*. This is also sometimes referred to as being in a *flow state*, and it is a place where our dreams can manifest effortlessly.

The opposite of that *flow state* is when you feel *stuck*. We all get stuck. If you ever get that feeling of being stuck you may be putting your energy in a place or places that aren't fulfilling you. Again, this isn't a *"good"* or a *"bad"* thing. If we didn't get stuck every now and then, we would miss out on opportunities to get *curious* and explore new possibilities for change. Curiosity can be a powerful tool for creating positive change and lead towards greater fulfillment. It's part of the journey as we shift from the 3D to the quantum realm.

When we get deeper into shadow work, you'll often find that it is in these *stuck* spaces that your repressed emotions are lurking, waiting to be felt, expressed, and brought back into your integrated holistic experience. At the start of shadow work it's important to not be so hard on yourself. The 3D linear model of thinking uses your past to create fear and anxiety about who you are and who you are meant to become. In quantum thinking, anything is possible! Through quantum thinking fear and anxiety literally become things of the past. You can leave them there.

So, why don't most people already quantum think? The ego and the shadow *"feel safe"* in what they know: the linear realm of consciousness, the stories about the past that tell them who they are. Even if these stories are holding them back and limiting their potential, they can feel familiar and comforting in a strange way because we "identify" with them. Many people are so attached to their past and believe they can predict the future based on what has happened before. The thought of actually bringing their dreams to life can feel *scary* because it would involve leaving the realm of the knowable and entering the uncertain realm of the possible. This way of thinking can cause people to avoid reopening old wounds or facing any potentially traumatic or chaotic situation.

So, like toddlers who refuse to let go of their safety blanket, people using linear thinking don't put themselves out there. As a result, their repressed guilt and shame (or other emotions) stay repressed. Their growth opportunities remain unrealized. Their broken hearts remain broken and closed off from the world around them. Again this isn't *"good"* or *"bad."* We're not here to judge. The goal is to *get curious, observe,* and *be open* to a new way of thinking and talking with ourselves, and creating a new dialogue with our shadow.

Not everyone is ready to change, and it is not our place to look down on others because they are not doing the work. It's always best to *be an observer*, and this is also the best way to begin working with yourself. Do not judge. That judgment could only be based upon the past. Instead of judging, be a wise observer of yourself. Imagine a wise elder watching a child play. You are both the elder and the child. Once you begin operating from this *child-like, creative, quantum state,* you will unlock greater potential for healing, loving, and fulfilling your deepest desires in life.

What Quantum Thinking is NOT

Waking up each day to the same life, doing the same things, thinking the same thoughts, having the same emotions…this is NOT *quantum thinking*. Being stuck in the same routine limits our ability to be fully alive and present in each moment. The shift to *quantum thinking* could be described as waking up to the present moment - no longer *sleepwalking* through life. Being fully present is often challenging, partly because living from the past is so addicting. We really, really identify with our past as though it's "who we are." The nervous system feels comfortable living the same routine, and the subconscious mind will sabotage efforts to shake up that routine. This creates a vicious cycle where past experiences (especially traumatic ones) keep us stuck in *linear thinking* - where low vibrational emotions run our lives. And we're doing it all completely unconsciously.

It is also quite common for people to project their own shadow onto others unconsciously. When someone is addicted to low-vibe emotions, they may see their own repressed emotions as coming from someone or somewhere else. It's "them, not me." This is the ego protecting itself from exposing our shadow or parts of ourselves we don't wish to examine.

For example, let's say I do something that "makes" you angry. If it was something really bad that justified your anger, then it would make sense to be angry. It's a different story when the anger becomes chronic. Some people become hormonally *addicted* to anger. As they go about their daily lives, their subconscious mind is tuned to a low-vibe, waiting for something to trigger that emotional reaction of anger. When that anger hits, these people also get hit with a small dose of adrenaline. Their physiology will crave this anger-adrenaline response, much like an addict craves their next hit of a drug. This rush is one example of how your repressed emotions can subconsciously run your life, and much of it is only possible if you're operating in a linear model of reality.

If you constantly get triggered and feel anger in different situations, is it coming from outside of you? Maybe there is an unresolved issue within you that's manifesting as other people or things "making" you angry. Looking for the source of your anger is the beginning of *shadow work*. For now, let's explore how we can observe whether we are operating from the *"good" and "bad"* linear mindset, or from a *quantum thinking* mindset. Recognizing how you are thinking will greatly help as you progress through this book.

Higher Mind vs. Lower Mind Awareness (Triune Brain)

Here's an important question to ask yourself often: Are you operating from your *higher* self or your *lower* self?

Buddhist philosophers, psychologists, evolutionary biologists, and neuroscientists have all described the mind (or brain) as consisting of three distinct parts. This is called the *Triune Mind* (or *Triune Brain)*. There's the part that handles basic survival (*reptilian brain*), the part that regulates emotion (*limbic system*), and the part that allows for higher-order thinking (*human neocortex*). To operate at the quantum level, it is essential to recognize which part of the brain is currently dominant. When something happens that triggers an emotional state, you are not as able to use logic and planning to make the best decisions. In the case of a frightening or traumatic event, you may even be triggered into basic survival mode where logic and reason are completely out the door and *linear* thinking is in control.

Another way to explain this is to use the example of The Matrix films. Are you getting stuck in the matrix of lower brain functions? Or are you like Neo in the films, (Neo means new), able to activate your *NEO-cortex* and use the power of your mind to escape the matrix? You can use your higher mind effectively to operate from the *quantum* model instead of allowing your lower brain functions to keep you trapped in the artificially constructed and limited matrix of *linear* thinking.

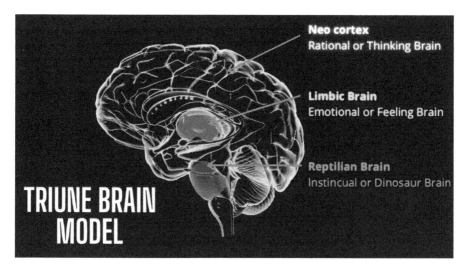

Reptilian Brain - Brain Stem - "fight or flight mode"

The brainstem located at the base where it meets the spine, is the first system to develop. This is actually a really valuable aspect of the brain in terms of survival. Without it we would not recognize when to run if a sabertooth tiger was chasing us. Most people are not being chased by tigers in the modern world, yet many people still get addicted to being in fight or flight mode. Being stuck in fight or flight mode can cause adrenal fatigue from the overstimulation, leading to emotional, mental, and physical burnout.

Limbic System - Amygdala - "Emotional Response"

The midbrain is where our emotions are managed. This part of the brain is important when it comes to our intuition, but when we are highly triggered, we can find ourselves using illogical thoughts to create our reality from this level of the mind. When people trigger us, our amygdala gets activated and all logic is out the door. An example is when you get angry and say things you never meant to say. That was you speaking from your limbic brain because the limbic system cannot see long term effects.

Human Brain - Neocortex - "Rational and Logical Thought"

The neocortex is our higher mind. As far as we know, it is unique to human beings. Through this part of the brain, we make logical thoughts. Have you ever tried to think logically while experiencing intense emotions? It's pretty tricky. That's why learning how to calm the mind so we can activate the higher aspects of the neocortex is not just important, but actually very valuable for operating at our highest potential.

This is why I use the analogy of *escaping the matrix* of the lower brain and activating the *NEO-cortex*. Many people around you in society, who haven't done this work, will be operating from the lower parts of their brain, the limbic and reptilian systems. Most people are completely unaware that they are doing it. If you've done the work and know how to recognize where your brain is, other people will not be as able to drag you into their lower-level *illogical & highly emotional* thinking. (This can feel like a super power once you make it a regular practice)

Let's think about money for a moment. Everybody loves having money. But do they love themselves? Money is a currency, and so are our thoughts. If you constantly live your life in lower brain's *fight or flight* mode, or in *emotionally triggered* thinking, you'll end up broke. You won't just be financially broke, but emotionally broken as well, because you are not in control of the real wealth which is the neurological currency of your own mind. (Remember time backwards is emit, it's not about time or money, it's ALL about energy which is the currency of connecting with your true self)

The goal here is not to make you less emotional or not feel things. The goal is to establish boundaries and know when you are operating from your rational mind or lower brain. Having this awareness also helps when others try to trigger or manipulate you. You'll be able to sense when it's best to stay in your logical mind or allow yourself to feel what they are presenting to you. It's important to both protect and understand how your emotions function. We'll explore this deeper in the *Emotional Mastery* and *Boundaries* sections of this book.

Section 2: Breathwork

(Please refer to my website, odysseymentorship.com, or YouTube channel, Odyssey Mentorship, for access to the Meditation/Breathwork Recording Links)

Now we will get into some physical tools to help you *quantum think*, *access your shadow*, and *decrease your stress* levels.

Why do Breathwork?

- Increase lung capacity, leading to new neural pathways in the brain

- Open nasal passageways and hyper-oxygenate the body

- Calm the mind, develop self-mastery, and cultivate a deeper connection between body and mind

- Access the theta brain wave state and reprogram the subconscious

- Open the nadi channels and eliminate blockages within the body

- Activate dopamine release from within

What does Breathwork do?

Breathwork stimulates and rewires the nervous system. If we are constantly in *fight or flight* mode, living in our reptilian brain, we can become neurologically addicted to the adrenaline released by the sympathetic nervous system. Like someone hooked on drugs, who's always craving that next hit, we can become hormonally addicted to the feelings of being stressed out. Breathwork helps to *rewire that connection* between the brain and body. This book's breath techniques help to stimulate the *vagus nerve,* which activates the *parasympathetic nervous system*. The *parasympathetic nervous system* is what drops us into *rest and relaxation* mode. This is extremely important. When you can access this space at will, you can get your mind and body to a place where they can calm down and heal yourself consistently.

Breath is the foundation for life and helps you heal because it puts your body in a relaxed state. As your breathing shifts, your neurology enters a place where you can consistently be tuned into your inner voice (and be aware of your shadow). When you do regular breathwork, it will be easier to *quantum think* and gain access to your shadow. You will no longer be physically and hormonally creating your experience based upon past traumas and experiences keeping you *stuck*. The more you do breathwork, the easier it will be. Just be patient and use your journal to track anything that comes up before, during, or after your meditations/breathwork.

When should you do Breathwork?

The best times for breathwork are first thing in the morning and shortly before going to bed. This is when your brain is either going into or coming out of delta (sleep) brainwaves. It is useful to be in this near-sleep state because the emotions you're attempting to access and the mantra you are utilizing, will have a deeper effect. Breathwork aims to relax your mind enough to get into *theta* brainwave state. We'll go over this more later in the book. For now, just understand that you enter theta brainwave state just before sleep, and this is when your mind is more programmable at the subconscious level.

Another great time to do breathwork is before a stressful event where you know you may be triggered, or after you've already been triggered and need to calm down. When you prepare your nervous system, grounding it and priming consistently with breathwork, you will literally feel a more electrical connection to your body as your neural pathways shift over time. You won't be as easily stressed, triggered, or affected by the external world and you will have the tools to remain calm when you do get stressed.

Meditations/Breath Techniques

(Included with this book you will get access to three meditations.)

Our primary technique is *Holotropic Breathwork*. The term *holotropic* means "oriented toward wholeness" or "moving toward wholeness" and comes from two Greek words - *holos* (whole) and *trepein* (moving toward something). So, *holotropic breathwork* means to work with your breath to orient yourself toward wholeness. Stanislav Grof, the pioneer of *holotropic breathwork*, describes linear thinking perfectly: "...in our everyday state of consciousness we identify with only a small fraction of who we really are and do not experience the full extent of our being." Holotropic breathwork can help you break out of that limited consciousness and unlock your unlimited potential within the quantum realm.

HOLOTROPIC BREATHWORK –

UTILIZING BREATHING INTERVALS AND HOLDING YOUR BREATH OUT TO ACTIVATE THE NERVOUS SYSTEM (15-20 Minutes)

This breathing exercise usually takes about 15-20 minutes. The goal is to do this meditation/breath technique *at least* once per day MINIMUM. You must have an intention or focus when doing this meditation. The focus can simply be calming yourself down if you're stressed out. Other times you may go into a breathwork exercise to work with your shadow. You could also use a mantra to create a space where you can calm down an overactive mind. This technique is a great meditation to do when you have a stressful day and need to chill out.

BOX BREATHING-

BASIC BREATHWORK INVOLVING CYCLES OF 5-SECOND BREATH HOLDS AND EXHALES. THIS IS THE QUICKEST TECHNIQUE TO CALM DOWN THE NERVOUS SYSTEM (3-5 Minutes)

Our second technique is a short exercise which is excellent if you're in a stressful situation and need a quick fix to relax the nervous system. *Box Breathing* is an ancient technique that is very simple. You exhale for five seconds, hold your breath out for five seconds, inhale for five seconds, then hold your breath in for five seconds. Repeat this cycle for a few minutes to relax the body/mind. The rhythm and cycles of breath have a profoundly calming effect.

SOMATIC BREATHING-

ADVANCED BREATHWORK/VISUALIZATION UTILIZED TO CREATE AN ALTERED STATE OF CONSCIOUSNESS FOCUSED ON RELAXING AND BREATHING INTO DIFFERENT PARTS OF BODY (25-30 minutes)

Our third technique is *Somatic Breathing*. *Soma* means "body" so it makes sense that this exercise is focused on calming down different parts of the body. We focus on going through each section of the body and getting out of your head to help connect, relax, and heal. Somatic breathing is a good meditation if you are sitting in the bath, lying in bed, or just relaxing by yourself.

Section Review

- Recognize the difference between *linear* thinking (being fixated on the past) and *quantum* thinking (seeing infinite potential in each moment).

- Realize that you can choose to shift from *linear* thinking into a new *quantum* reality.

- Use your awareness to identify triggers, limiting beliefs, your inner critic, and self-sabotaging habits. Get curious and see what's coming up for you.

- Use the quantum model of thinking to identify low vibrational vs. high vibrational thought patterns.

- Understand that quantum thinking is a SUPER POWER and shifts the way you perceive time. Your past no longer creates your future. Your future holds infinite potential.

- Remember the story of the Chinese Farmer. Are things really *good* or *bad?* Maybe.

- Become familiar with the Triune Brain model as a road map to understand where your mind is operating from in different situations. Are you using logic? Emotions? Or are you in the reptilian brain of *fight or flight* mode?

- Use *breathwork* to connect with your *shadow*, calm the nervous system, and develop a deeper connection to your body as you sift the unconscious mind.

- Make a regular schedule to tune into your body with meditation/breathwork. Begin rewiring your subconscious mind and shift the flow of your energy. Gain access to your shadow/repressed emotional energy so you can start moving toward wholeness. Begin rewiring your subconscious mind and shifting energy in the unconscious to access your shadow/repressed emotional energy and begin bringing it back online.

Shadow Awakening Workbook
(Use your journal or write answers here.)

Cultivating A New Mind: Quantum Thinking

What is the *Quantum* model of thinking, and how does it differ from *3D Linear Newtonian* thinking? (We want to make sure this is clear in your mind)

_____

_____

_____

_____

In what areas of your life are you still stuck in the linear model of consciousness, where things are either *good* or *bad*? (Remember the story of the Chinese farmer.)

_____

_____

_____

_____

What could be possible for you to operate from the quantum model? (How will you use your *Quantum Thinking* superpower?) Make a short list below…

_____

_____

_____

_____

Where I am stuck in *Linear* thinking—What do I deserve in the *Quantum?*

_____

_____

_____

_____

Triune Brain & Shadow Work GOLD

Do you understand how to *escape the matrix* of the lower brain functions and operate from your "Neo" Cortex? Where in your life do you find yourself falling into the matrix of the lower brain?

_____

_____

_____

_____

When our amygdala gets triggered, we fall into the emotional limbic system, and when we are highly triggered, we can get caught up in the Reptilian Brain of "Fight or Flight" mode.

Remember, feeling emotions is neither *bad* nor *good*. It's just that there are more options and possibilities available to you when you are operating from your neocortex. You want to be using your higher brain functions as much as possible, especially when making BIG decisions in life.

The GOLD at the end of the tunnel of shadow work is recognizing when/where you are triggered and learning how to not fall into the *matrix* of the lower brain functions. When you have mastered this, you will also be able to recognize when others are projecting their shadow onto you and won't be as easily affected by it.

Higher Self Quantum Reality

Imagine yourself in the near future, where you've been consistently operating from your highest self. **What does that feel like? What does that look like? Where do you see yourself, or who do you see yourself becoming by the end of this shadow awakening work?** Please write a few sentences below to clarify the outcome you are creating.

_____

_____

_____

_____

Odysseus Andrianos

Breathwork

Make sure to check out the three breathwork exercises included in this chapter. The best time to do them is early in the morning, before bed, and preceding or after a stressful event. What days/times will you schedule for your breathwork or meditation practice? Note them below:

Mon

_____

Tues

_____

Wed

_____

Thurs

_____

Fri

_____

Sat

_____

Sun

_____

HOMEWORK

Schedule some time each day for your inner work practice

1. Begin integrating breathwork once per day. Choose between *Box Breathing* or *Holotropic Breath* depending on your timing. If you have more time to relax, then do the *Somatic* breath.

2. Identify the mantra to use during your practice (examples below).

   "I am loving awareness," "I am worthy of healing," "I deserve financial abundance."

   "I deserve to love and be loved," "I forgive myself and honor my healing journey."

   Repeat these mantras when doing your breathwork or meditation practice to effectively plant the seed in your subconscious mind.

3. Begin to identify the causes of emotional triggers and how they keep you stuck (examples below).

   A family member or friend does not respect your time and energy, so you go back to self-sabotaging eating.

   A co-worker is not respecting your boundaries, which contributes to you creating limiting beliefs around your self-worth.

   A TV program or advertisement triggers a fear response, so you fall back into thoughts of anxiety.

4. Make sure to let loved ones know that you are doing inner work and healing.

Questions to answer before moving on to the next section of the course:

What parts of yourself do you not want others to see?

_____

_____

_____

_____

What are you afraid of becoming?

_____

_____

_____

_____

What feelings are you avoiding?

_____

_____

_____

_____

What things in life do you desire or feel you truly deserve? (Get clarity, write them down, and allow them to manifest.)

_____

_____

_____

_____

*"Shadow work is letting go of who you should be,
so that you can be who you actually are."*

—Christie Inge

CHAPTER TWO

Section 1: Shadow Work: Rediscovering Our Light

There are many layers to *shadow work*. The primary goal of this book is to do three things:

1. Provide you with tools to access your shadow, manage your emotions, establish boundaries, and teach you how to use these tools effectively.

2. Give you the confidence to handle whatever comes up when accessing and integrating your shadow (including repressed trauma stored as emotions).

3. Awaken your infinite potential by accessing repressed emotional energy and harnessing it to heal, while learning to use your shadow as a guide rather than a saboteur.

What is *Shadow Work*?

Shadow work is when we begin to access repressed aspects of the self that are buried deep within the unconscious mind. Some examples of these repressed aspects of the self include: repressed emotions, traumatic memories, and physical or emotional abuse we may have experienced early on in life. There may be many of these painful experiences lurking within the unconscious mind. These past programs may manifest in the present as self-sabotage, self-hatred, or even abusing our loved ones and ourselves.

Why does this Happen?

These limiting (and sometimes harmful) behaviors occur because the unconscious mind is where our ego creates barriers to protect us. These barriers prevent us from seeing how our past traumas run our lives. They can result in poor eating habits, excessive gambling, and addictions to drugs, alcohol, sex, and money. They can also keep us in a state where we reject our ability to truly love or trust ourselves and others.

This brings us back to the *linear* vs. *quantum* models of thinking. When we repress our emotions, it actually rewires our egoic mind to cause us to continually seek out and re-experience the same emotional stimuli. Even if we are consciously aware that we're being abused or abusing ourselves, the subconscious mind's neurologic belief is that we are experiencing "love."

For example, someone who experienced parental abuse as a child may subconsciously associate that abuse with love. Parents are supposed to love their children, so the unconscious mind links the abuse to the desired love, attention, or approval that the child was seeking from the parent. Later in life, they will seek out that same "feeling" of love in the form of abuse, and which is done unconsciously. This pattern will continue until the person is ready to work with their *shadow* to access these repressed emotions and the corresponding energy within the body.

Here's an example of how shame and love can become unconsciously linked:

Imagine being a young child and seeking love from your parents. Instead of receiving love, your parents use shame as a means to control your behavior. (This is likely a pattern passed down to them from their parents) Unconsciously, we will seek out shame in future relationships because our shadow associates that feeling of shame with love. Consciously, we will wonder why we continue to experience shame in our relationships. On an unconscious level, our shadow is still attracting the experience of shame because it equates it with love. Until you have faced your shadow, and integrated the repressed energy of shame, the same patterns of shame-seeking will continue to occur unconsciously. Releasing ineffective patterns is WHY we do shadow work.

The Inner Critic & Limiting Beliefs

The *inner critic* is that little voice in your head that pops up here and there as you go about your day. It is the *linear thinker* lurking in your unconscious mind. It speaks to you from your past and limits your available responses to each situation you encounter by creating blinders that keep you from seeing things objectively. Sometimes it can show up as mind chatter that sounds like a broken record on repeat, saying the same things over and over again. It can also be a consistent flow of self-sabotaging thoughts, like an IV drip of *limiting beliefs*.

Examples of Limiting Beliefs:

"I'm not good enough."

"My feelings aren't valid."

"I'm not worthy of love."

"It's all my fault."

"I'm stupid or ugly."

"I'll never have enough."

"I'm a victim."

Past childhood traumas (and even limiting beliefs passed down to us from our parents) can quietly dictate the course of our entire lives from our shadow or unconscious minds. Working with our shadow helps it start becoming aware of that voice and creating a new dialogue that satisfies your shadow's needs, so your shadow becomes your guide instead of working against you.

Imagine this: You have this aspect of yourself called *guilt,* and instead of allowing yourself to acknowledge and deal with this emotion, it gets stuffed into your unconscious mind. The more you ignore it, the bigger it gets. The guilt just wants to be expressed. It just wants to be felt. As you continue to push it out of your conscious thoughts, not allowing yourself to feel it (because you fear the pain), this unfelt emotion continues to grow bigger and stronger within you. This guilt may even shift or morph into *anger*, or possibly even *rage*, all because you won't allow yourself to feel it.

Over time that repressed emotion of guilt starts running your life. You get angry at yourself or project your anger onto others, and either don't realize you're doing it or don't know why. That deeply embedded emotion of guilt (or whichever emotion is not being acknowledged) just continues to grow, causing more pain and dysfunction within your life. This will keep happening until you are ready to make a shift.

This deeply repressed emotional energy can even cause physiological health problems. The repressed anger turning to rage can become so deeply ingrained within our physiology that we begin to experience heart or blood pressure problems because we are using up so much energy to not allow ourselves to express this emotional pain. This is why shadow work is crucial to our mental and emotional health but also our physical health as well.

How Do We Begin the *Shadow Work* Journey?

Shadow work is unique to each person's experience, but it generally begins with discovering what emotion or emotions you have been repressing, suppressing, or denying. Unearthing emotions is where the digging begins.

The best way to find which emotions you've been repressing is to recognize what things are triggering you on a regular basis. Start asking questions like: When do you get emotionally triggered? Why does it trigger you? What's creating mind chatter in your life? What is your inner critic REALLY telling you? What's your shadow not allowing you to see? This is the place to get curious and create an "access point" to discover the true *core conflict*. (More on this in a moment.)

The greatest version of ourselves is hidden in our shadow. This means that you will love yourself more fully once you've gone through the process of working with your shadow. Instead of your inner critic sabotaging you, it will become your guide. Most importantly, you will begin to see when other people are *projecting their shadow* onto you. This will keep you from taking things personally because you understand that other people's behavior is a reflection of their internal state of mind. It's important to realize that after doing this work that you will still trigger other people, but you'll have the awareness to know how to maintain a healthy relationship with others despite their flare ups because you've done your inner work.

Shadow Identification

Identifying where your shadow shows up becomes easier as you progress with your inner work. It's like lifting weights - like the neurons fire and activate the muscles with each subsequent workout, it gets easier to progress with your training. What you'll begin to notice as you start doing inner work is that your shadow will attempt to distract you, usually by making you look somewhere else. Often, the thing we want to work with the least and avoid is the repressed emotion or trauma that we need to access the most. Our shadow doesn't want us to see whatever we've been shoving deep down inside our unconscious minds. It is trying to protect us. But that protection is preventing us from becoming our greatest selves.

Initially, when we are identifying the shadow, we are examining the areas in our life where we have repressed energy, emotions, or trauma. These are often the areas where we are not feeling fulfilled. A great way to identify the shadow is to stay on top of your breathwork and meditation game. With a calmer mind and nervous system, you will notice when the shadow pops up and tries to run the show or take you off track. A calmer state of mind helps you to more easily identify triggers and limiting beliefs when they arise from the unconscious. This is also a great thing to watch for when you're setting goals for yourself. Take note of how your shadow could redirect you and send you completely off course from where you actually intend to go. In some cases, this could be a place where we are having an internal argument with ourselves on an unconscious level.

Accessing Our Inner Child

For many of us, the emotional or traumatic experiences that shifted our lives happened at an early age. These experiences which the *limited, linear mind* wants to assign as "negative" can actually become *access points* to our greatest healing. To cultivate the healing process, we must be patient, compassionate, and very gentle when we are accessing our deepest wounds.

We cannot approach the shadow with aggression, or be too much into our masculinity (we'll go over gender principles more in the *Boundaries* section). We must allow ourselves to soften up to communicate with our inner child. Consider approaching your shadow in the same way you would approach a small child. Aggression is never the answer, extreme care and empathy are key to creating a new dialogue with our inner child. Imagine a wounded child, for example Bruce Wayne from the *Batman* stories. As a young boy, he witnessed his parents being killed right in front of him. You would probably be gentle and speak softly if you approached a young Bruce Wayne knowing what he had just been through. It's the same when you begin working with your shadow. Hopefully you can see that when you access your shadow, this is NOT a place to rush things or show up with the intention to control the show. It's actually a place to surrender to its needs and listen to your intuition. When you are able to listen quietly, calmly, and deeply to what these repressed aspects of yourself have to say, you will gain access to healing in ways you could have only imagined.

This is the place where we can open up our hearts and feel what we felt like before the trauma happened, or who we were before the external world (traumatic experience) started running the show. When we first come into this world, we have no knowledge of these things called *emotions*. As we try to figure them out, we may be ridiculed or shamed for expressing them, but as children we don't even really know what emotions are. Once we are able to feel deeply into our hearts, we can find that space of who we were before the trauma occurred. Then we can begin to change our story and love ourselves again. This is the journey to access our shadow and begin to reframe our past experiences.

To put it simply, all your inner child really wants is to feel listened to, cherished, and nurtured. Once you can quiet your mind enough, you will be able to feel your way into this heart space where you can create a new inner dialogue of loving your whole self including your inner child. In order to get to this space, it is important to know how to listen to these repressed emotions or shadow aspects and be open to hearing the naked truth of what the shadow needs to heal. Your inner child already knows what it needs, and as you progress through this book you will gain more tools to open your heart and listen more deeply.

How do you Implement Shadow Work?

We mentioned curiosity earlier, and it will keep coming up throughout this book. Get curious about your triggers because they are clues to discover your "core conflict."

Here's a visualization trick that can be very helpful. Think about a time when you were really triggered when someone or something "made" you really angry or upset. What were the thoughts and feelings that kept repeating in your head? (You know, the thoughts or limiting beliefs that you clung to tightly to justify feeling so triggered.) Picture those thoughts and feelings as your linear thinking security blanket. You felt the need to hold on to them in that triggered state. Now imagine there's a loose thread coming from the corner of that security blanket. Start pulling on the thread by using the power of your curiosity. What will you find? Continue pulling at it until you reveal the real "core conflict." So, what is it? What is the "real" problem that was holding you back? Pulling that string is often difficult. The shadow wants us to feel safe and comfortable by keeping that core conflict hidden under the security blanket. But with persistence and curiosity, you can unravel even the most tight-knit of blankets. This unraveling will allow you examine your barriers and blocks held within you and set you free from the chains of your limiting beliefs.

Oftentimes, we have to sift through the unconscious mind to find the deeper "core conflict." It may take examining many triggers for us to eventually figure out, which is why journaling and keeping a record of what comes up is so crucial to your long-term performance in shadow work. It's like keeping detailed records for your business or bank account. If you don't keep proper records, how will you know what your business needs to succeed? If you're not on top of your finances, how will you know if you're about to go broke? (Side note: You don't need to track everything, but definitely write down the BIG stuff or things that repeatedly come up to go over it later in meditation when you can properly process those emotions.)

Working with the shadow can also be like massaging a knot out of a muscle. This is a great comparison because unprocessed emotions will eventually show up in the physical body if we repress them long enough. When massaging a knot, especially if it's very dense, you need to work at different angles and find the access point to really get deep in there and release the muscle tissue. The issues are in the tissues, muscle tissues. You'll know when you find it because there is usually a noticeable shift in the way you feel. Just like releasing a knot in your muscle allows greater blood flow to the rest of your body, releasing those emotional knots will allow a greater flow of your emotional energy and make it easier to move through life's ups and downs.

Approaching the Shadow

First and foremost, be very gentle and honor the fact that you are doing this work to heal the most wounded aspects of yourself. In this space, you may find yourself having an argument with yourself internally. During these conflicts, your shadow may attempt to offer up distractions to keep you from seeing your wounds. Whatever "fears" come up may be a distraction that your shadow is creating to prevent you from seeing the real things you need to heal. It can get messy, but your mess will become your message. Or, we could say your crap becomes fertilizer to plant new seeds of personal growth.

To support the healing process, you must focus on your basic physical and emotional needs. This book is not about teaching you how to have a perfect diet, but it is still important to get super clear, clean, and focused on your diet including the quality and quantities of food. Proper nutrition will ensure that you have the mental clarity and energy necessary to keep working with your shadow. The word "diet" comes from the Latin word *dieta,* meaning "Way of Life." Think about the way your life is going. Do you want it to change? Your diet may be a place where your shadow is showing up. Changing your diet can be a powerful step in changing your way of life. Proper gut health is actually a big part of proper mental health.

In Taoist philosophy your stomach is related to the earth element and people who struggle with their diet are often using food as means to keep themselves grounded. But this is "false grounding," it's really just a coping mechanism because you're lacking the proper awareness around how the foods you are eating are affecting your gut health. Often this coping mechanism is you unconsciously feeding your repressed emotions and this is how a lack of awareness can cause disease.

Are you unconsciously sabotaging yourself with your diet? Are you regularly getting enough water to flush out the toxins from your system? Here's a great visualization to use regularly. When you're in the shower or bath, imagine that you are also washing away any old or stagnant energy that might have become stuck to you. Make sure you set time aside for regular breathwork, meditation, or both. It's also imperative that you get plenty of sleep to allow deep inner healing. Take notes of any BIG dreams or images that come up in your sleep. These can provide clues to follow in your shadow work journey. The dream world is a great place to gain insights into the unconscious mind and how it might be affecting our daily lives.

In the waking world, make it very clear to your friends and loved ones that you are going through the healing process. This can be as simple as saying, "I am in the healing process, thank you for respecting my journey." This healing process can actually be a great conversation starter and a way to begin establishing new boundaries with the people in your life who may have triggered you in the past. We will go over this more in the Boundaries section, but for now, think about establishing a "container" for your healing process by verbalizing it to others and acknowledging this space within yourself. They need to know to keep an eye on you while also providing the necessary space for you to do your inner work. Communicate with them ahead of time to maintain your most important relationships. Be clear on who is crucial to your mental and emotional well-being and who is not.

Uncharted Territory

Deeply feeling your way into this healing space may seem foreign and uncomfortable at first. This is perfectly normal. As you begin sifting through the shadow to find your inner gold, it can sometimes feel like traveling uncharted territory without a map or GPS system to guide you. Most of us don't have an active relationship with our shadow. We're not used to looking into our triggers for the access points to healing.

Sometimes, what we think are our "positive" traits may actually be our shadow hiding right in front of us. For example, some people think that working overtime and collecting extra money is "good" for them. But excessive work may be a sign you're masking a deeply embedded trauma and not allowing the time necessary to rest and heal. Another typical example is mothers who are constantly giving to everyone around them. They are taking care of everyone else…but themselves. They may think this shows they are a "good mother," but in reality, they may be rejecting their own health and much-needed time to recharge. No matter your situation, you can't perform your best, feel your best, or be in a place to receive the love you deserve if you aren't taking the time to also care for yourself. Balance is key and specifically being honest about where you are out of balance is how you heal and create a new life for yourself.

It is in this uncharted territory where you must let go of what your subjective mind wants to think and allow that inner intuitive voice to be your guide as you feel your way into this space. This is where you become more aligned with your higher self and tuned into your intuition. You can begin working on your repressed energies to bring them back online, fully loving yourself in unimaginable ways.

Stirring the Emotions

Shadow work involves dredging up deeply embedded emotions, and as mentioned before, it can get messy. It's totally normal to experience what's called "brain fog," as you start this process of inner work. Brain fog can occur as you begin working with your repressed emotions. As you start to reintegrate your shadow and reprogram the old operating systems that do not honor who you are truly meant to be, it can create a feeling of uneasiness, like you're no longer standing on solid ground. It's okay to experience brain fog. There may even be a couple of days where you just struggle to get your normal things done. Remember that your mess becomes your message. The more clear you are about your intentions, the easier it will be to stay on the path to success. Continue to use the power of your curiosity as you go deeper into the journey of awakening and integrating your shadow.

Section Review

- Identify what shadow work is and how to begin working with repressed emotions, trauma, and energies in your unconscious mind.

- Recognize how and why emotions become stuck in your unconscious mind and how you can begin accessing this energy to make an internal shift.

- Keep track of your triggers, the meaning you're creating from those triggers, what emotions are showing up, and how to go deeper into what may be going on below the surface in your mind.

- The beginning of shadow work is accessing your inner child. Be gentle and compassionate, and more than anything, LISTEN to what your shadow's needs are.

- Use your triggers (and emotional red flags that pop up) as a way to get curious. Like finding a loose thread, get curious and keep pulling on that thread to get down to your "core conflict," - the emotional energy that is REALLY creating the problem.

- Approaching the shadow is much easier if you do regular breathwork, meditation, and consistently connect with your body and emotions.

- Be willing to let go of old ways that no longer serve you. When stirring the emotions, allow your emotions to become your guide. Use the tools from this book to journey into the abyss of your awakened potential in the shadow realm.

Section 2: Rediscovering Our Light: Shadow Work

What is Shadow work?

Let's begin making the unconscious...conscious. The goal here is to dig into the darkness of the shadow to find our GOLD. The shadow is 90% gold & only 10% darkness.

Triggers & Limiting Beliefs

What are the things that trigger your inner critic to appear? Identify any limiting beliefs & "mind chatter" thoughts that hold you back.

(Please list them below or write them in your journal.)

Limiting belief examples: "I'm not good enough," "I'm not worthy of being loved," "I'm a victim."

<u>Triggers</u>	<u>Limiting Beliefs</u>
_____	_____
_____	_____
_____	_____
_____	_____

Inner Child Connection

What trauma did you experience during your childhood and how is it affecting your life today?
(Reflect here and use this as an opportunity to dig deeper.)

_____

_____

_____

_____

Approaching the Shadow

As you work with your wounds, remember to be gentle and compassionate with yourself. Find the loose thread and use the power of your **curiosity** to keep pulling at it until you get to the root of the issue or the **"Core Conflict."**

Keep in mind that when we work with the Shadow, it is **NOT LOGICAL.** Keep writing down anything BIG that comes up. You have to feel your way in there, so be patient with the process.

Implementing Shadow Work

Whatever fears you may have could be your shadow distracting you from seeing the "real thing" that's holding you back. Also, remember that some of your so-called **"positive traits"** may be your shadow hiding right in front of you.

List any fears or positive traits that may be holding you back. (Example: Being an overly nurturing person who takes care of everyone but never makes time for yourself.)

_____

_____

_____

_____

HOMEWORK

(Schedule some time each day for your inner work practice.)

1. Be clear on what your shadow is, so that you'll know when it shows up to take you off course or back into old ways of being or self-sabotage.

2. Track your triggers and the meaning you're creating from those triggers. These are clues to what's going on below the surface in our minds.

3. Use your triggers to "**get curious**" so that you can begin negotiating with the shadow and satisfying its needs. Listen to your shadow and acknowledge it so you can start healing.

4. Allow your emotions to become your guide by tapping into your intuition. Let your shadow become your guide rather than your saboteur.

5. Keep up with your breathwork and meditation practice. Use your mantras to plant positive seeds within your unconscious mind.

Questions to answer before the next section of the book:

Identify limiting beliefs, thought patterns, and mind chatter? (Use triggers as clues.)

_____

_____

_____

_____

Recognize any repressed, suppressed, or denied emotions you haven't been allowing yourself to feel. How has this created self-sabotage in your life?

_____

_____

_____

_____

Begin working with your inner dialogue as you identify your shadow. How is it showing up in your conscious world?

_____

_____

_____

_____

Have you let others know that you are going through the healing process? Please do this.

_____

_____

_____

_____

What goals do you have? How could your shadow send you off course?

_____

_____

_____

_____

"To confront a person with his shadow is to show him his own light."

—Carl Jung

CHAPTER THREE

Section 1: Shadow Integration: The Shadow Revealed

What is *Shadow Integration* and How Does it Differ from *Shadow Work*?

Shadow work is the beginning, when we first acknowledge the shadow and then sift through the darkness (unconscious mind) to uncover repressed or suppressed emotions and denied aspects of ourselves.

Shadow integration is when we start to work with these repressed aspects of ourselves and integrate them back into the conscious mind. This is when we can really start to heal our deeply embedded (and previously hidden) emotional trauma.

How do we integrate the shadow?

First and foremost, we must center ourselves and be grounded. The best way to do this is with some breathwork and meditation or time in nature. The goal is to calm down the logical mind and go from the mind chatter state of beta brain waves into the near-sleep state of theta brain. This allows for greater access to the subconscious mind.

(We touched on this in the Breathwork section of Chapter 1, and we'll go over this more when we discuss Emotional Mastery in Chapter 5.)

The subconscious mind only works on images. When we allow the logical, analyzing mind to calm down and stop the constant flow of words, we can begin to access the images used by our subconscious minds. We can even shift those images and shape how they are used to guide our lives.

The key here is to create a space where we can cultivate self-compassion, which allows us to transmute lower vibrational emotions such as anger and fear into higher vibe emotional energies like love and curiosity. The first step in this transmutation is creating self-awareness. Take time to check in with your body. Spend time in nature. Physically tap different parts of your body and feel what thoughts and emotions come up for you. Consistently practicing your breathwork and meditation will make it easier to tap into your shadow. If you can do this out in nature, with lots of prana energy (oxygen) moving through your body (or *nadi channels),* you may find it will be easier to calm the nervous system.

When working to integrate your shadow, it can be challenging to allow yourself to be completely honest about emotional traumas from your past. The uncomfortable topics that we struggle to be honest about - even with ourselves - are actually the ones that will set us free the most. When we examine our trauma, we can find new ways to access them that aren't so BIG, or ugly, or painful. We can learn to love even our most painful experiences, and to appreciate them for helping shape us into who we are today. This is where we create a new dialogue and change the stories we tell about ourselves. Reframing our trauma is what allows us to love ourselves more fully as we transition through the integration process.

What does NOT Integrating the Shadow Look Like?

It is actually very common in modern society to NOT have done the work to integrate the shadow. We live in a world where expressing yourself with an open heart has become taboo. Being vulnerable is often viewed as a weakness. Sharing your feelings may be frowned upon when it could be disruptive to the well-being of a corporation, company, or even a family unit. Many of our repressed childhood traumas are repeatedly triggered by living within our modern society. This is a large contributor to the mental and emotional health crisis facing society today. Is this a "bad" or "good" thing? Neither. The *quantum* model of consciousness shows us that it's just an opportunity to observe things for what they are - information which we can sift through in order to discover new opportunities and new ways of being.

When we do NOT integrate the shadow, it shows up as consistent self-sabotage, poor eating habits, excessive consumption of drugs and alcohol, and sexual problems. We'll use any stimulus necessary to avoid facing our inner wounds and unconscious mind. The unintegrated shadow will have us abusing ourselves mentally, physically, and emotionally - all while not even being fully aware we are doing it!

When we continue to repress or suppress an emotion over time, it can show up like an inner demon controlling our lives. It's not an "actual" demon, but that doesn't mean it's any less powerful. Have you ever been really triggered and got very angry with someone, only to realize later that it wasn't that big of a deal? This could be an example where your shadow is covering up a repressed or suppressed emotion. That unacknowledged emotion will show up like a demon, controlling your life with anger or even rage, if you do not "do the work" to examine and integrate the repressed energies back into your experience.

When our shadow is running the show, we don't recognize how it is programming and conditioning us. We don't see how it is making us resistant to change. We can't see the triggers that are keeping us stuck in the same old behaviors. We may even become unconsciously addicted to a way of being that is sabotaging us.

Here's a brief example: A client of mine had a family member pass away. This family member had a ritual of always eating cake on Sundays. To honor and maintain a feeling of connection with this relative, my client adopted this cake-eating Sunday ritual. On a conscious level they were honoring their lost relative. But they were also destroying their health and developed diabetes as a result. The client was not aware that eating cake was a coping mechanism for losing their relative, and it was not helping to heal from the trauma of the loss. Many people will take on traits or habits from their parents or loved ones and reenact them in their day-to-day lives. It becomes an automated aspect of their psyche and they are not consciously aware why they are behaving this way. They can literally "identify who they are" with their traumatic past, which runs their life unconsciously. Some people have allowed the shadow and these unconscious identifications to run the show for 10, 20, even 30 years, not knowing why they are so miserable.

"Until you make the unconscious conscious, it will direct your life and you will call it fate."

—Carl Jung

Not integrating the shadow can affect you in a multitude of ways. You may struggle with receiving money, or not allowing yourself to process emotions, or have fears of opening your heart to receive love. You may use addictions to mask your true potential. The repressed energy hidden by your shadow may be limiting your confidence to move forward in your career, or it could be causing serious health problems because you are not really deeply loving yourself. All this can show up simply because you have rejected "feeling" certain emotions that just want to be felt and expressed through you. This is how repressed emotions can appear like our inner demons.

Imagine a part of yourself has been ignored, rejected, or maybe even hated...How would you feel and react if you were ignored, rejected, and hated? An aspect of yourself may not have received the love you felt you deserved as a child, so you continue to deprive yourself of that love as an adult. That's an inner demon running the show right there, but the so-called "demon" is just the unconscious aspect of yourself showing you where to find the repressed or suppressed emotion. It's actually a guide showing you where you need to heal if you can only listen compassionately to it. Instead of being a demon it becomes more of an angel, when you change the angle you choose to see your shadow from. It's honestly just a subtle shift in your awareness that leads to your greatest healing and the dawn of your greatest potential.

The important thing to remember is that from a quantum level, none of these things are necessarily "bad," or "good." They are simply *ways of being* that can be completely shifted IF you are willing to do the work, get curious, face the uncomfortable parts of yourself, and feel your way into the healing process. There's never been a better time to fully love yourself than right now! The world is ripe for change, and that change starts with you and your healing journey.

How do we work with repressed emotions and how do we integrate them?

The first step is very simple, and by now you should already be doing this. First, accept the existence of the shadow. Just this alone can be a relief to some people because they are finally acknowledging the work they need to do and the wounds they have ignored. Second, discover what the qualities and intentions of your shadow are. And finally, start negotiating with your shadow so you can fully begin the healing process. It is in this space where you have initiated yourself into your own healing journey. From here you will begin to notice subtle changes in your experience as you bring the shadow back online and integrate that repressed energy back into your experience.

1. **Accept the shadow.**

2. **Discover the wounds and work to be done.**

3. **Negotiate with shadow to satisfy its needs and allow healing to begin.**

Take your time with this process! Allow yourself plenty of time to feel what's coming up within you. Enjoy the process and know that these inner emotions are really just aspects of yourself that just want to be acknowledged, felt, and expressed. Oftentimes in doing this work, we find different layers to accessing this shadow space and one emotion may lead us to another, which is why patience and compassionate awareness are crucial in this work.

Benefits of Shadow Integration

Improved relationships - You will be much more in-tune with your emotions and your triggers, which will make you more aware of when you may be triggering others. You will also be able to identify when other people are projecting their shadow onto you, which may be the greatest benefit of shadow work.

Clearer Perception - Before engaging in shadow work, you may have had anxiety, depression, or other low vibe dense emotions running your life because you've repressed or suppressed those emotions. Imagine how clear and effortless things will become when those blockages are removed from your experience.

Enhanced Energy and Physical Health - Not only will you have more energy to exercise, but you will also love yourself more. You will be excited to exercise and eat healthy because of the deeper connection with yourself.

Psychological Integration & Maturity - Your ability to call yourself out on your own bullshit will create more confidence. Being aware of your inner critic, limiting beliefs, and how repressed emotions can sabotage you. This makes it nearly effortless to stay focused on your dreams and keeping your mind in the right place consistently.

Greater Creativity - You understand how to work with your masculine and feminine energies (we'll go over this more in the boundaries section) in such a way that you can move into a creative space from a quantum perspective. This allows you to be in a space where you can manifest your reality rather than being stuck in the old linear model of thinking where things "happen to you." Also, you may eventually notice how others are clinging to their linear reality and not seeing the same results as you.

Deep Inner Loving - The final goal of shadow work is loving yourself more completely. You're no longer living in the false light because you've integrated your shadow into your whole being. You've accepted your shadow and allowed it to be your guide, rather than your saboteur, so you can show up more authentically in every aspect of your life.

The Gatekeeper

When working with the shadow and integrating these repressed emotions, we may come up against some barriers. When we mention the "gatekeeper," we are talking about an aspect of the psyche that is blocking you from creating the access point to some of your deepest wounds. What this means is that an aspect of your ego (or shadow) is protecting you from seeing your trauma.

When we face the gatekeeper, things can sometimes get a little foggy (this is where brain fog can show up). Your mind will attempt to distract you and keep you from seeing the "core conflict," or wound, that is holding you back. Sifting through the shadows can take a different amount of time for each person, and as mentioned before, **do not rush this process**! Honor your healing journey, and remember that in the end it's all about loving yourself more to become who you were always meant to be.

A great way to perceive the gatekeeper is to imagine yourself as a traveler in the darkness of the unconscious mind. You suddenly come to a bridge that has a BIG grumpy troll blocking your path. In order to cross this bridge, you have to answer a series of questions. If you answer correctly, the troll will allow you to pass. The troll may actually be an aspect of yourself you've repressed to protect your wounds. It needs to know you're really ready to face your wounds or trauma, or it won't let you pass. So don't stress out, get angry, or anxious if you're not gaining access to your shadow quickly. You may just need to sit with your shadow for a bit and sift through what's there. Be patient, poised, and compassionate as you work with the gatekeeper and delve deeper into your shadow.

When we work with the shadow, it's important to realize that it is NOT logical. We are sifting through the unconscious mind where the trauma has been stored as a shape or a blob. Imagine how an abstract artist may interpret emotions on a canvas and that may give you some idea of what may show up in the unconscious mind. This blob or shape (which is really just energy) is just an interpretation of how a past experience is stored within us. Once we have accessed this energy, we can begin integrating or shifting it from within ourselves, deeply healing ourselves from within.

An example of a gatekeeper could be someone who cannot allow themself to cry. They were told as a child that it's not safe to cry, not show their emotions and if they did, they were weak or worse yet, even punished for expressing themselves. The gatekeeper in this instance would be the shame surrounding being vulnerable and expressing emotions. Often one of the simplest and greatest things we can do is just let our emotions out. The act of crying is a physical representation of the release of energy. When you cry, your body - which is made of water - is letting go of the abstract energy held within us in the form of pain, anger, grief, sadness, aggression, worry, and a wide range of other emotions.

An excellent way to process and integrate our emotions is to keep our bodies moving. Exercise, dance, yoga, Qi Gong, and any other type of consistent movement will help you move any stuck energy from within the body. Choose an activity that you find to be fun and use it as a tool to keep you grounded in your body and move any stagnant emotional energy that is keeping you from healing.

Not releasing our emotions is often the root cause of dis-ease. Is it a surprise that the leading killer in America is heart disease? It likely has a lot to do with NOT feeling our emotions. Just think about the word "e-motion," energy in motion. It really comes down to keeping your body in motion. If you are experiencing blockages, it will be hard to move properly or express yourself authentically. People with deeply repressed emotions will have joint problems that prevent them from moving freely or properly. This is why shadow work is so crucial to your overall health and well-being.

Reframing

Okay now we are getting to the juicy stuff…The goal of going over this with you is to share multiple ways to manage what may show up in the shadow work process so you are physically, psychologically, and emotionally prepared.

Once we have discovered the repressed emotions or aspects of ourselves, we can begin the *reframing* process. What this means is that you are reframing an image from your past that your unconscious mind identifies with. This will help you to shift your personification of who you are today instead of identifying with your traumatic past. Did that make sense?

When we experience emotional trauma from our past, it can become a BIG image in our minds. This can get stuffed into the unconscious, where it can affect much of our lives. But when we reframe that BIG image from our past, we can make it smaller and more manageable, which allows us to finally heal from it.

By examining the traumatic experience in new ways, you are able to see it from new perspectives that you were not aware of or conscious of at the time of the traumatic experience. This reframing of the experience CAN shift the storyline of the 3D third dimensional linear reality that we've created based upon past experiences. This shift allows us to move our current day experience into a quantum model of infinite potential. Essentially you are becoming a time traveler, because as you shift attachment to the past it alters your future. Shifting your timeline and more importantly your energy allows you to have a more fulfilling life experience because you are no longer carrying the baggage from the past. When we have effectively reframed the past and broken free from its chains, it allows us to love ourselves fully and manifest the life of our dreams.

3-2-1 Shadow Reframing Process

This is another example of how to implement the reframing process in order to shift trauma from the past and create a quantum future with infinite possibilities. (This is an excellent exercise to do in your journal.)

Choose what you want to work with: an experience, a person, co-worker, or family member you had strong emotional challenges with or who was abusive towards you.

3 - Imagine the experience in 3rd person - Imagine the past experience, the person or persons, and even yourself as if you are an observer watching it happen. Describe the qualities of this experience (tone of voice, facial expressions, body language) and any other characteristics that stand out to you. Write this down in your journal and even verbalize the experience if this feels right to you.

2 - Speak to them in 2nd person using your language - Now imagine reliving the experience from your perspective. Ask questions like: "Why are you doing this? What happened to you? What are you teaching me?" Write down the questions and answers and even verbalize the experience if this feels right to you.

1 - Become this person, 1st person - Use statements to describe the emotions (anger, rage, guilt, shame, or grief) that they are feeling and what they are experiencing. Write this down and even verbalize the experience if this feels right to you.

Throughout this process, take note of any disowned qualities within yourself that may have been created by the experience. Allow yourself to experience any traits you may have projected onto the other person. Now you can reintegrate any repressed or suppressed emotions created by the experience, which allows you to love yourself rather than repressing the emotion coming from this past experience. Because you have now created an access point to let go of the emotion, you are no longer operating from that linear timeline. This may need to be done more than once to fully manage and process the trauma you have experienced. You may need to repeat it for the same experience and incorporate it in different ways for other experiences. If you need extra support to fully grasp and implement this, please reach out for support.

My Email: odyandrianos@gmail.com

Section Review

- Identify the difference between *shadow work* and *shadow integration* and how to access the shadow vs. how to integrate repressed energy of the shadow.

- Practice integration of the shadow through a range of exercises to calm the nervous system. Relax into "theta" brain wave state and begin working with your subconscious mind to manifest a new reality.

- Understand the dramatic impact of an un-integrated shadow. Our repressed emotions can show up like a "demon" because the unacknowledged energy in our unconscious mind needs to be expressed and integrated.

- Working with repressed emotions requires acknowledging our shadow, caring for and addressing its needs.

- Integrating the shadow provides a wide range of benefits, most notably being able to love yourself more fully and deeply. This is because you are no longer repressing an unfelt aspect of your psyche. So now you actually have access to fully love yourself.

- The gatekeeper can be an aspect within the unconscious mind that blocks access points to our repressed emotions.

- Reframing allows us the ability to create a new timeline shifting away from past experiences affecting us today. The reframing process allows us to see things "as they are" rather than identifying with who we were when the trauma happened.

- The 3-2-1 process is a model of reframing that creates new access points to our past stories by seeing them from 1st, 2nd, and 3rd person perspectives. Feeling our way into these different personas helps to shift our attachment away from identifying with the emotions from our past stories.

Odysseus Andrianos

Section 2: The Shadow Revealed: Shadow Integration

Shadow Work vs. Shadow Integration

Shadow work - The beginning process of accessing the shadow to find repressed aspects of ourselves and emotions hidden in our darkness.

Shadow Integration - When we've begun to integrate the repressed aspects of ourselves back into our psychology and heal our emotions.

How often have you been doing your meditation/breathwork?

_____ days per week

What emotions, recurring thoughts, stories, or limiting beliefs have come up for you?

_____

_____

_____

_____

Shadow Integration

Now that we've done the work to access the shadow, we can begin to integrate it. Remember the three steps to integration:

1. Accept the existence of the shadow.

2. Find out the qualities and intentions of the shadow.

3. Begin negotiating with the shadow.

Often what we call our shadow is a repressed or suppressed emotion which is an "aspect" of ourselves that we have left in the dark.

The key question to ask is: "**What does it need to heal?**" This is the initiation process to integrating the shadow.

When we work with our shadow it will reveal our path to healing, but we must be willing to sit with it and listen to what its needs are so we can cultivate a new relationship.

What are the qualities and intentions of your shadow? What does it need to heal?

_____

_____

_____

_____

The Gatekeeper

The gatekeeper is an aspect of ourselves that blocks us from accessing our wounds.T his is where brain fog can creep in and prevent us from seeing the **"Core Conflict"** that needs healing or needs to be addressed.

Keep in mind that the shadow world is **NOT logical**! It's abstract, like a blob or a shape. It's energy stored in the unconscious mind. This energy is dense, and as you work with it you can release it and move out of the 3D to the quantum as we mentioned in section one.

If you are struggling with integrating your shadow, imagine what ways your gatekeeper could be distracting or holding you back. Could there be something deeper that you are not seeing?

Please list below what could be showing up or distracting you:

_____

_____

_____

_____

Reframing

Just like taking an old picture and putting it into a new frame, we can take our old stories and limiting beliefs and change how that image shows up for us in our conscious world.

Please list what story or image you would like to change in your life:

_____

_____

_____

_____

3-2-1 Shadow Reframing Exercise

Take the story or image you listed above and utilize it in this exercise below, or choose what you feel you would most like to work on. (For example, a family member, coworker, friend, or old story you're still holding on to.)

3: Face it - Imagine looking at the experience from a 3rd person perspective, as if you were watching it as the observer. Write down what the experience looked like:

_____

_____

_____

_____

2: Speak to them in 2nd person - Relive the experience and use your own language. Ask them: **Why are you doing this? What happened to you? What are you teaching me?** Add any questions that feel right for you and write down the answers below:

_____

_____

_____

_____

1: Become this person - Use statements to describe how they are feeling. See if you can find any wounds that they may have been passing on to you, and notice any disowned qualities within yourself that you may have projected onto them. Notice any emotions that show up for you and write them below. They will create an access point to your healing.

_____

_____

_____

_____

Take some time to reflect on what shows up for you in this exercise.

_____

_____

_____

_____

HOMEWORK

(Schedule some time each day for your inner work practice)

1. Keep working with your shadow to identify any repressed or suppressed emotions or stories that are still holding you back unconsciously. Work on creating a new dialogue with the shadow. **Are there other shadows you have not examined?**

_____

_____

_____

_____

2. What are your shadow's needs? Are you satisfying those needs so that your shadow can feel safe to allow you to progress towards healing?

_____

_____

_____

_____

3. Make sure that you are being authentic and honest with yourself as you are sifting the shadow realm on your path to healing.

4. Make sure to keep up with your breathwork/meditation practice, mantras, and making physical and mental health a priority in your life.

Questions to answer before the next section of the course:

What images from your childhood could you or would you like to reframe?

_____

_____

_____

_____

Can you sit with your inner child and listen to what it needs to heal?

_____

_____

_____

_____

What would it feel like to fully love every aspect of yourself unconditionally?

_____

_____

_____

_____

Have you been maintaining your breathwork or meditation practice?

_____

_____

_____

_____

Odysseus Andrianos

"The journey of self-discovery is not always an easy path. Understanding the light that you are & also being able to acknowledge your shadow self, you will begin to understand that both are crucial in this physical world."

— Stefania Love

CHAPTER FOUR

Section 1: Shadow Awakening: The Dawn of Human Potential

The Shadow Awakens

We call this section the "Dawn of Human Potential," because that's what an awakened shadow feels like. Your greatest human potential arising from within you, just as the darkest night turns into the brightest day. Could you imagine if everyone on the planet was invested in this type of work, if everyone went deeper into who they really are, why they feel emotions, where they feel emotions, and worked on integrating their repressed energies, rather than simply projecting and acting upon them? For just a moment, I would like to commend you for doing this work! It is not easy but the more you do it, the easier it gets from the standpoint of knowing the fundamentals to go deeper into yourself and shedding layers of emotions, trauma, or even generational wounds passed down through families. Thank you for your courage.

I also would like to highlight that everyone works with their shadow at their own pace. Even though this is the shadow awakening section, some of you may not be at the stage of awakening your shadow yet. The goal here is to prepare you for what is to come on your journey, so your logical mind can handle what may arise while doing this work in the unconscious. It can be a different journey for each person, but by the end of this course you will have the fundamental tools, a strategy, and a game plan to sift the shadows to find the gold within you. Keep in mind we are working with the unconscious, so we can never be fully sure of what will arise from the unconscious mind. When something really traumatic occurs, especially in childhood, those memories are often repressed or suppressed. When doing shadow work, it's not uncommon for very dark repressed emotions, like memories of physical or sexual abuse, to come to the surface for healing. If you need support, always reach out to a professional therapist, doctor, or experienced coach/guide to support you.

Acknowledgment

The final piece to the shadow awakening process begins with gratitude. We begin by acknowledging the work we've done thus far, the energies we've shifted, and changes we've made within ourselves. Even if you are still just beginning to access the shadow, and you're just sitting with it for now, that is a HUGE accomplishment!

So, whether you're just becoming aware of your triggers, beginning to work with your inner critic and limiting beliefs, integrating the shadow, (or maybe you've even moved to a new layer of emotional shadow work altogether), acknowledgement is part of the vibration that allows you to love yourself for doing this work. The reason why acknowledging the journey is so crucial is that the wounds and repressed aspects of the self can only be healed once we have acknowledged their presence.

Wounded Healer

Acknowledgment of our inner wounds is like keeping a finger on the pulse of our healing journey as we go deeper into ourselves. It has been said that "the path is the medicine," and as we work with our emotions it frees up our ability to feel the path leading into a new life by creating a new experience from within. The path to inner work is about becoming your own healer, loving all aspects of yourself, and being more intimate with your wounds. This intimacy with your wounds is what establishes a stronger bond with your innermost self. The beauty of this is that as we cultivate inner trust, this will eventually be reflected in our relationships with others as well.

To heal literally means to "make whole." As we work with our inner wounds, the acknowledgment is what creates freedom from our 3D linear past. This awareness is what sets us free to establish the life of our dreams. This is what makes it possible to show up authentically because we are no longer operating from an unconscious state. As Carl Jung states, "We've made the unconscious, conscious." This consciousness is where we fill in the gaps to become a whole and complete person transmuting our wounds and inner pain into a life we've always deserved. Here we can see the dawn of a new potential within us.

The Dark Knight

We touched on the origin story of *Batman* in the first section of shadow work and we need to hit it again because it's such a great analogy for approaching your shadow. When working with wounded aspects of your inner child, it's like finding a young Bruce Wayne (*Batman*) just after his parents were killed right in front of him. This may sound like a harsh comparison, but this is a way of explaining to the logical mind what it can be like to go through the process of accessing the shadow and integrating your emotions. The most wounded parts of yourself may not be ready to be felt or integrated. So once again, I cannot stress this enough, feel your way into this space with the utmost compassion and patience. Imagine what it would feel like to have an open heart as you embrace your inner child and embrace your inner wounds.

The inner child may be a representation of repressed emotions like shame, guilt, anger, or sadness, but when it shows up in the unconscious realm it may appear more like a blob or an odd shape. Remember that this is the unconscious world. It's NOT logical. It's abstract. The real question here is this: "IF your shadow is not ready to shift or move...can you just sit with it, nurture it, heal it, and most importantly love it?" Patience, poise, and compassion are crucial on the path of healing.

This repressed emotion has been waiting so long for you to feel it, to express it, and just be with it. Maybe all it wants at first is just for you to BE with it. This may be scary at first. This inner child, this wounded aspect of yourself, might be a little "upset" that you've ignored it. Wouldn't you be upset if someone ignored you? Well, this aspect of yourself that you've been completely ignoring is your *shadow self*. The more you can love yourself will determine your success with the shadow, so open up your heart and love yourself BIG! Get curious and listen. The more love you have for yourself, the more it will also show up as loving relationships in your external world - as within, so without.

Healing the Inner Child

If we dig deep enough, we often find some trauma that occurred early in life (formative years). When we rediscover the moments from our childhood that are still affecting our operating systems today, this is often the jackpot of *shadow work*. Can you recognize areas of your life where you may be showing up as a wounded child? Some of us have had a relationship (or maybe more than one) where we *consciously* thought we were seeking love, and instead, we kept getting wounded (or even sabotaging ourselves). This could be the shadow *unconsciously* projecting itself - showing us where to look. This is where we must continue to get curious and sit with ourselves to find the "root cause" or "core conflict" that is hidden within us, just waiting to be acknowledged and expressed. What emotion is not being expressed? Could there be a deeper emotion that is waiting to be experienced? Authentic curiosity is the key to unlocking our infinite potential here.

Shadow Projections

Once we begin to *integrate the shadow*, we can recognize the inner critic showing up as a friend instead of a foe - a guide, rather than a saboteur. By becoming acutely and cognitively aware of when we are projecting our shadow onto others, we also begin to recognize when others are projecting their shadow onto us. Here we find the gold nugget at the end of the tunnel in shadow work.

This may have already happened to you in your past, where you become fully conscious that someone is attempting to relive their childhood traumas through you. They put you in a role as an actor in their *subconscious* reenactment of an experience that left them wounded. They haven't done the work to heal their emotional pain so they will unconsciously relive it through you so they can get a high from their repressed shame, anger, guilt, and/or sadness. They will blame you for their inner emotional pain and this is simply their shadow projection so they can unconsciously keep protecting the wounded part of their psyche. This is a great place to work on our compassion for others, remain empathetic, and use our awareness to maintain the relationships we truly care about.

It's important to remember here that you may be the one triggering them into this reenactment. You can only be conscious of this if you first become aware of your own shadow (and your own triggers). Otherwise, you may end up falling into what is known as the "demon dance," where you and the other person's shadow begin an entirely unconscious reenactment from your pasts. The shadows dance up a storm, and you're left to pick up the mess left behind. We can see this play out in relationships where the same energy and arguments keep arising consistently and there is no progress or growth. It's just a mindless cycle of the same "effects" without proper investigation into the root "causes."

Soul Gardening

In order for a seed to grow, it must be planted within the dark soil and then nurtured. When we do *shadow work,* it's like tending to a garden within us. The *soil* is our *soul*. Placing our *heels* on the ground connects us with the earth and helps *heal* our hearts. Regular electrical grounding (along with the other exercises we've gone over like breathwork and meditation) can help to rewire our nervous systems and allow us to better transmute our emotional energy. Your soul cannot manifest the fruits of growth and success until you've dug deep into the soil of your soul and nurtured the seed of your own wounds with the love, compassion, and forgiveness that **you deserve**.

People wonder, "Why isn't my life changing?" Well, often before the branches of a tree grow, we must first deeply nourish its roots and these roots grow in the darkness much like the work we do with our shadow. Just as a garden won't appear overnight, it is important to be patient and allow yourself to deeply feel your emotions. This is what sets you free: loving ALL aspects of yourself (even those repressed in your own darkness). Shame, guilt, despair, self-hatred…these emotions may feel like crap, but that "crap" becomes your fertilizer. You are literally turning crap into new life. Remember, "*Your mess becomes your message.*" Nothing is either "bad" or "good" from the *quantum* level of thought. Be confident as you cultivate the seeds of a new you and emotionally feel your way into who you were put on this earth to be. This is what we mean by, "The Dawn of Human Potential."

Unconscious Somatic Trauma

Many of us may not realize that long term repressed trauma can actually get stored in our physiology, in our muscle tissue. Our muscles are a memory bank and our nervous system keeps us hard-wired to respond to external stimuli (triggers). Do you remember learning how to do something that required muscle memory? For example, learning to ride a bicycle requires lots of repetition until you get to the point where your muscle memory takes over and it no longer requires your conscious attention. It's the same way with chronic emotions that get lots of repetition.

If you look at people who suffer from chronic depression, or people who are constantly staring at their phones, their body becomes physiologically adapted to a certain posture. The hormones created in these states will affect the nervous system and neurological wiring of the body. The subconscious mind doesn't recognize positive or negative. It just goes with what it knows. Intense emotions that are felt deeply enough (or often enough) will get stored in both the unconscious mind and the physical body. Much like riding a bike, your body learns to move based on feeling (or suppressing) your emotions…especially the BIG emotions. "E-Motion" is **energy in motion**. So, if you don't allow yourself to "feel," there could be emotional blockage in your body. If you have chronic pain or injuries that affect your movement and doctors can't find the answer, it may be coming from repressed or suppressed emotions held deep in your physiology that have yet to be processed, examined, and fully integrated.

Here's an example below of how this works

Trauma>>>Mind>>>Emotion>>>Brain>>>Hormones>>>Body

When we experience trauma (mental, physical, emotional, or spiritual), our mind processes the trauma into an emotion. The emotion triggers our brain to produce hormones based upon the emotions we felt. The body can actually become physiologically addicted to the hormonal responses to depression, anxiety, anger, rage, etc. (we literally get a high from it). This occurs due to the hormonal "hit" we get when our emotions are translated and expressed from the brain to the body's experience. Repetitive hits of the same emotion producing the same hormonal response create a chemical concoction within the body that lights up the nervous system like sugar or cocaine. The body will seek out the response to anger, rage, or sadness, and the craziest part is that we won't even know that it's happening. When we let our shadow run the show from behind the scenes, we will consistently and unconsciously engage in the same sabotaging behaviors and failed relationships and call it "fate." We will continue to look for something externally that's "making us" angry or sad or anxious, when it's actually coming from within.

When the shadow is running the show, it tries its best to keep us stuck in *linear thinking* and prevent our rational mind from seeing how our hormonal and physiological addictions are limiting our lives. And what's really crazy is that this can go on for decades or even an entire lifetime as long as the trauma or emotions remain DEEPLY repressed and unintegrated. This can lead to chronic *dis-ease* and even the adrenal burnout of our sympathetic nervous system as we are constantly operating in "fight or flight" mode, battling against a world we are projecting from within ourselves.

Sometimes our shadow does this as a protection mechanism. For example, people who are addicted to gambling or making money will keep getting a dopamine hit when they win a big hand or realize a large financial gain, but it will NEVER satisfy the inner child who has been waiting all this time to be loved, nurtured, and healed. This is why some of the most wealthy, famous, and successful people still never feel FULLY satisfied. Our addictions may show up as an external manifestation of internal suffering. They are often an unconscious representation of our self-hate and our rejection of deeply loving ourselves (especially our inner child/shadow).

The part of us that we hate (or refuse to fully love) creates repressed emotional energy. This will continue to affect the physical body until the shadow that has been waiting to be expressed and felt is released from the prison we created for it within ourselves.

What Does an Awakened Shadow Feel Like?

Work with the shadow to release your repressed emotions, trauma, and inner wounds. The long-term effects include:

- Your inner critic becomes your inner guide. You tune into your *higher self* for guidance rather than letting your repressed emotions run the show and sabotage your success.

- You gain a much clearer vision of your future, which is based upon "what is" rather than fighting against or trying to avoid "what was," and you get rid of any limiting thoughts or beliefs that no longer serve you.

- You DEEPLY love ALL of yourself, even the aspects which were repressed for years, and you start to feel like a whole/complete person (possibly for the first time ever).

The journey begins and ends with the process of self-discovery - finding out who we truly are and who we're meant to be in this world as fully-integrated souls living here on Earth.

An Alchemized Mind

The awakened shadow is an *alchemized* mind and body - when the left and right hemispheres of the brain are firing in harmony with each other. The process of alchemy always begins with the distillation and purification process. In many cases, this is a process of being reborn. As we let go of parts of ourselves that are no longer serving us, it can literally feel like a death and rebirth. This is where the essence of who we are starts to shine as we integrate these wounded and ignored parts back into our psyche. This is what's known as *transmutation* - when our shadow is integrated.

The HEART is the bridge that connects the mind and body through this alchemical process. Shadow work is the path back to our hearts, because our heart is where our home is. My father, who was a sound mixer, always told me that the word "heart" contains both "ear" and "hear." This reflects our ability to deeply listen to what is needed in order to heal because when we bridge the mind and body through our hearts, we feel deeply grounded and connected to our golden path in life.

As the shadow awakens, we realize that who we once were is just a string of stories we were holding onto, and often those stories are based upon unexamined wounds. It's like we've been limping through life, and doing it for so long that we don't even realize it anymore. In these situations, we often use drugs, alcohol, TV, porn, video games, gambling, or any other means of numbing our pain as a crutch to help us get through a difficult period of life. In the short term, these vices may not appear threatening, but in many cases the temporary crutch can become a habitual handicap of addiction. Vices are precisely where the inner demons of our repressed emotional pain lie dormant within us. Instead of directly facing our demons, we use different substances or stimuli to numb our pain, often leading to a slippery slope of self-denial and self-destruction.

When we've done this work to awaken our shadow, we genuinely see the dawn of human potential within ourselves. We get back all that energy we were wasting to repress our emotional pain, which can now be used in more meaningful ways as we apply it to becoming our most authentic selves. We can live in harmony with our hearts and create the life of our dreams with far greater ease. The transmutation of our shadow into gold is what this journey is all about. **Every ounce of effort is worth its weight in gold!**

Section Review

- *Shadow awakening* is the "Dawn of Human Potential." Instead of repressing our emotions and trauma and hiding from our true nature we begin to heal from within and evolve as human beings.

- The shadow awakening process works for everyone at their own pace. There is no rushing this process! *Be patient* with your healing process.

- Acknowledge the journey you've taken thus far, and realize that *the path is the medicine* as you heal your wounds from within.

- Remember the example of *the Dark Knight* (Batman). Be sure to gently feel your way into the shadow space as you work with repressed aspects that you may not have allowed yourself to feel in years.

- When working with your *inner child*, listen to what needs must be met and be aware that things may come up that you weren't aware of when you first started this work.

- Take note of any areas where you are still *projecting your shadow* or where your shadow could still be sabotaging you with old programming. Recognize how you could also be triggering other people's shadows to show up in confrontations.

- *Gardening the soul* means digging deep into the soil of the heart and cultivating a new world where you can deeply love all aspects of yourself unconditionally.

- Chronic repressed emotions can show up in our bodies and cause *dis-ease*. Trauma could run our lives and rewire our physiology to become addicted to the hormonal response.

- An *awakened shadow* can let go of repressed emotions and trauma. Once we are able to love ourselves fully, the shadow becomes our friend and guide, and our relationships will flourish because we are more comfortable in our own skin.

Section 2: Dawn of Human Potential: Shadow Awakening

Acknowledging the Journey

By this point, you've acknowledged your shadow and begun the integration process, or at least you've started integrating some repressed/suppressed emotions back into your conscious awareness.

Remember, wounds can only be healed once we've acknowledged them. *"The path is the medicine."*

What wounds have you been working with and how is the process going for you?

_____

_____

_____

_____

What changes have you seen as a result of working with your shadow? Are you finding it easier to love yourself more now? Please reflect below on what's changed for you and the shifts you've noticed in your life.

_____

_____

_____

_____

Healing Our Inner Child

The jackpot of shadow work is rediscovering the traumatizing moments from our childhood that are triggering our behaviors today. These triggers can help us find where we are unconsciously sabotaging ourselves or projecting our shadow onto others.

We have now begun awakening the shadow. **Are there any places in your life where you still find yourself showing up as a wounded child?** Please write down what's coming up for you as we dig a bit deeper into the shadow realm of childhood.

_____

_____

_____

_____

Shadow Projections

As we work to integrate the shadow, we will begin to notice where other people may be projecting their shadow onto us. We must first be clear on where we are still projecting. We must be conscious of our own shadow before seeing it in others.

What emotions do you find yourself projecting onto others? What trauma could you be reliving in these relationships? Example: Do you often find yourself getting angry or sad and blaming it on others? This could be a direct mirror into yourself and the places you still need to work on.

<u>Emotion</u>	<u>Childhood Trauma Being Re-lived</u>
_____	_____
_____	_____
_____	_____
_____	_____

Unconscious Somatic Trauma

Our bodies can become hormonally addicted to our trauma, which can lead to the experience of physiological pain as our nervous system becomes rewired to the stimulus.

Are there any areas in your body where you feel you've been storing emotional trauma or wounds? Please list any areas where you've been experiencing chronic pain that you feel is associated with holding onto emotions.

_____

_____

_____

_____

The Conscious Awakening

What does it feel like to have an awakened shadow? It feels like having a new friend, as our shadow becomes our guide instead of being our saboteur. When we've acknowledged our shadow and negotiated with it, we can begin to create the life we've always **deserved**.

As we awaken our shadow, our chosen future will become clearer and easier to manifest. **What does the future you deserve look or feel like to you?** Please reflect below.

_____

_____

_____

_____

HOMEWORK

(Schedule some time each day for your inner work practice.)

1. Identify when and where you are projecting your shadow onto others.

    _____

    _____

    _____

    _____

    _____

2. Identify when and where others could be projecting their shadow onto you.

    _____

    _____

    _____

    _____

    _____

3. Consistently imagine what your life will feel like as you live with a fully awakened shadow.

4. Make sure to keep up with your breathwork and meditation practice, reciting mantras, and make physical and mental health a top priority in your life.

Questions to answer before the next section of the book:

What emotions are still showing up for you, and is there still a dominant emotion you are still repressing? (Examples: anger, guilt, hate, sadness, or rage.)

_____

_____

_____

_____

Which behaviors are you still struggling to change in your life?

_____

_____

_____

_____

What is the primary trigger that keeps you going back to the same behavior(s)?

_____

_____

_____

_____

When you feel really good in your life, what emotion(s) feel dominant?

_____

_____

_____

_____

"Knowing others is intelligence. Knowing yourself is true wisdom. Mastering others is strength. Mastering yourself is true power."

— Lao Tzu

CHAPTER FIVE

Section 1: Emotional Mastery: Law of Polarity

How do we Heal our Emotions?

Healing our emotions really comes down to one simple concept: feeling them and transmuting them. The key word here is "transmutation." What this means is to transform and mutate from one form to another. As we shift our emotional energy, it changes from a fixed, linear, 3D, particle-like nature to a quantum, wave-like nature. Like all things we wish to change, transmutation begins with *awareness*. We will not be able to change if we lack awareness. What's strange is that this has become a foreign concept in modern society. Most of our society lacks awareness, which is often portrayed as desirable "Ignorance is bliss." Most of us have been programmed to bury our emotional pain into the depths of our unconscious mind or shadow. Living in "ignorant bliss" has become so normalized that many people are completely unaware of how to manage their emotional pain. This leaves them suffering mentally, physically, emotionally, and spiritually.

We are unable to *feel* and *process* our emotions when we push them out of our conscious awareness. All this unresolved energy gets stuck within our physiology. Over time, this stored emotional energy builds up and starts festering. This can leave us feeling drained, emotionally burnt out, and even lead to dis-ease. The key to healing these emotional wounds is to hold yourself in a mental state of "*compassionate awareness.*" Have empathy for yourself on this healing journey. Instead of ignoring our emotional pain, we must honor it. Honoring our pain means creating the space to express it, feel it, and release it. This is what I mean by *transmutation*.

One great challenge that many people face during the emotional healing journey is a lack of proper support. Very few people are equipped with the tools to offer support during this journey. Most doctors are not *trauma-informed,* and few therapists actually go deep enough to release the emotional pain held dormant within us. Ultimately, whether you hire a doctor or a therapist or a coach, you are the one who must implement the tools and hold yourself accountable for doing the work on your healing journey. At the most basic level, our emotions are just energy. When our stored emotions are released, we are able to tap into an immense and deep wellspring of nourishing and healing energy.

This is a huge piece of the GOLD that comes with shadow work. As we cultivate a relationship with our shadow, we are able to develop a new and refreshing relationship with ourselves. We can set ourselves free from the shackles of our painful past, and in doing so, we open ourselves up to create a new future with *unlimited potential.* We discussed moving from the 3D to the quantum model of consciousness in Chapter 1. The 3D model represents a degree of being *unconscious* because we cannot create anything new from this level of thinking. In fact, we could say that linear thinking is nearly completely lacking awareness because of the inability to see the limitless possibilities available at the *quantum* level.

Someone who has acknowledged and integrated their shadow (and awoken to their infinite human potential) has achieved *emotional mastery.* It is much easier for this person to operate from the *quantum* level of awareness. This level of awareness is what creates the potential for a limitless life. This level of awareness is required so that we can recognize our triggers and how they lead us astray with sabotaging thoughts, beliefs, habits, and behaviors. When we cultivate this higher level of thinking, we stop wasting energy by repressing or suppressing wounded or dissociated aspects of our psyche. We begin to balance the inner *Yin* and outer *Yang* nature which gradually extends outwards, creating a natural balance and harmony in our lives. This harmony and attunement of the mind, body, and heart is the essence of *emotional mastery.*

What is Emotional Mastery?

Emotional mastery begins with understanding the Law of Polarity that all opposites connect and dance with one another. Let's think about "hot" and "cold" for a moment. There is no specific point where "hot" ends and "cold" begins. They are different degrees of the same thing, temperature. The same holds true for "anger" and "love" which are different degrees of the same emotional energy. When we have the awareness to know what emotions we are experiencing, and remain mentally calm enough to be aware of what the opposing emotion would feel like, we can actually *transmute* one emotion into another. This is valuable when we are faced with situations that are highly stressful or when emotions are running high.

As we progress through this section of the book, you will learn how to identify your emotions, discern what part of the brain you are operating from, and begin to recognize how your brain waves are affecting you. We'll also go deeper into how to calm the mind and actually rewire it for higher performance when you are emotionally triggered.

Why Emotional Mastery?

Chronic low-vibe emotions can lead to dis-ease. We've already talked about how being stuck in "fight or flight" mode can burn out our adrenal glands. Over time, chronic stress can also lead to a wide range of other health conditions including heart disease, hypertension, cancer, hypothyroidism, and too many others to list here. Instead of allowing chronic low-vibrational emotions to run our lives, we can adapt and rewire the brain to *polarize* and *transmute* our emotions when appropriate.

Learning how to *polarize* and *transmute* your emotions is an excellent tool for when you get triggered. It essentially comes down to using your emotions or letting your emotions use you. If you're not in touch with your emotions, you may make irrational decisions when triggered into the limbic system's "fight or flight" response of the reptilian brain. It's important to remember from the quantum level that experiencing these emotions is neither "good" or "bad." At the most basic level it's all just energy, and you can harmonize your body with these emotional energies to keep yourself from burning out.

When you are "tuned in" to your emotions, you will experience less stress, depression, and anxiety. You'll have more empathy for others, which results in deeper relationships and higher quality communication. This all occurs because you learned to master your own energy first. When you are presented with things externally, they will have less chance of taking you off track because you are able to tune into your internal guidance system (your higher self). Your logical and intuitive brain will be working in harmony, as if your body and mind were a musical instrument, connected together through your finely-tuned nervous system. This is what emotional mastery feels like. When you are vibrating at such a high frequency, you can move through life freely, confidently, and effortlessly. Essentially this is known as "flow state."

Polarity of Emotions

Like the Yin and Yang of Taoist philosophy there is a polarity to our human experience. This polarity can be seen in our emotions below. Awareness of how to polarize our emotions is a crucial tool to navigate our everyday lives. Below is a short list of polar emotions:

FEAR VS. FAITH

HATE VS. LOVE

SELFISH VS. GENEROUS

ANGER VS. PATIENCE

CRITICISM VS. SYMPATHY

GREED VS. KINDNESS

WORRY VS. HOPE

HYPOCRISY VS. COURAGE

VANITY VS. ASPIRATION

Learning the art of polarizing our emotions is essentially a form of *alchemy*. This process of mental alchemy involves the *transmutation* of energy into its opposite. Carl Jung referred to this process as "Enantiodromia," the changing of something into its opposite. This is a means of shifting our emotional frequency to prevent our emotional energy from getting stuck, which can often be the root cause of disease.

This list of opposing emotions above comes from a doctor named Thurman Fleet. He claimed that one of the biggest mistakes medical professionals make is not addressing emotions when they diagnose physical conditions. When doctors do not take into account the emotional energy of the patient, they may prolong or even prevent the healing process by continually attempting to fix the physical condition or "effects" rather than addressing the emotional root "causes" of the problem. Over time, this can even lead to mental health problems. The patient thinks, "There is something wrong with me. Why can't my body heal?" When in reality, the underlying cause of emotional trauma was never addressed or never even examined in the first place. The cause is what creates the effect.

Let's consider someone who suffers from depression and slouches constantly. Their shoulders sulk which leads to back problems. They go see a chiropractor or doctor which is still a great way to relieve symptoms, but the doctor never asks them about their emotional pain. They continue to receive adjustments and "treatments" that only work on the physical level. Until the underlying "cause" of the emotion manifesting as depression is addressed, it is highly unlikely the patient will see the long-term healing they are seeking. When we address the *cause* (emotions), it shifts our energy and creates a space where the *effect* (healing) can take place. This works differently for each person depending on their experiences, the diagnosis, and what shift needs to take place.

The list includes basic emotions that people experience each day. The reason for going over this list is so that we can recognize which emotion is being experienced and identify its polar opposite. By continuing to cultivate emotional awareness, we become able to polarize our emotions. By being aware of the opposing emotion, it will be easier to find balance and avoid getting stuck in intense low-vibrational emotions.

Inquiry can be difficult at times, especially when we get triggered, but this is an excellent tool if you find yourself suffering from our even addicted to low vibe emotions. For example, if you are feeling fear, you can bring your conscious awareness to the fear and ask: "Where can I find faith in this situation?" When you find yourself getting angry with someone, ask: "How can I find the patience to calm down?" If you feel yourself hating someone, ask: "What aspects of this person can I love?" If you still aren't very clear yet on what low-vibe emotions are, we'll go over them more in this section.

Just like with shadow work, when it comes to mastering or polarizing your emotions, you have to be keenly aware of what you are feeling. By mastering the awareness of feeling your emotions, you'll be able to shift your experience with less discomfort. Emotional mastery can also help you maintain boundaries as well. It's important to also note here that when we do this, we are NOT repressing an emotion (especially if it's a big emotion). You should take a note of it on your phone, and then write it in your journal later to process and go over what comes up. Keeping these records helps you prepare for future challenges and your ability to process what came up. This tool of polarizing your emotions is especially valuable in situations where it is challenging to express your emotions at that moment, or if someone is attempting to trigger you into a reactionary state. Polarization is particularly valuable when engaging in difficult conversations with people we love, like family and friends, who hold highly charged energetic emotions and have differing beliefs than us. Use these challenging conversations as an opportunity to grow by utilizing the tools you've learned in this book to give you confidence and clarity.

Emotional Mastery of the Triune Brain

We already went over this in the *Quantum Thinking* section of Chapter 1, but it's so important that we are going to briefly touch on it again here because it DIRECTLY relates to emotional mastery.

If you recall, there are three levels of the brain. The first to develop was the brainstem that handles basic survival and responds with "fight or flight." Next, we have the "emotional center" which is the limbic system, and finally we have the higher or rational mind, the "Neocortex."

A great way to remember this is to stay in your Neocortex, and out of the MATRIX of the lower brain functions. In other words, awaken NEO, your neocortex. This means when you see other people who are highly emotional, you can recognize that their amygdala has been triggered. They are now in their limbic system, and all logic has gone out the window. When we see others who are exceptionally highly triggered and falling into their reptilian brain "fight or flight" mode, we can avoid letting them drag us down into our lower-level brain functions.

As we cultivate emotional intelligence and the awareness of how our emotions function and how they show up in our bodies, we can also begin to recognize which level of the (triune) brain we are operating from. As we become aware of how our neurology works in conjunction with our mind, body, and heart (emotions), we gain long-term value of not wasting buckets of energy and ruining relationships with people (including ourselves).

A KEY thing to remember is that you must recognize how your brain is operating and which level of the triune brain it's operating from before you can be fully aware of where other people's brains are operating from. If you're highly emotional or in fight or flight mode, how can you think logically? Remember the analogy of the matrix, awaken NEO (your Neocortex) and be aware when others try to drag you into the emotionally triggering MATRIX of the lower brain functions.

It's important to note here, we're not saying that feeling emotions is a bad thing. It's just that being in the throes of emotion is not the best place to be

Odysseus Andrianos

when we need to make logical decisions that could deeply affect our lives and future. We want to be able to navigate these different levels of the brain effectively for peak performance. Navigation is especially true when dealing with other people who have not done their inner work and may get highly triggered. Sometimes you may trigger someone else unintentionally. You're no longer talking to their rational mind; you are talking to their shadow. Being able to spot when this happens is one of the gold nuggets of shadow work because you'll begin to see how other people's shadow could be running their lives.

Vibration and Frequency

Everything comes down to energy - where the mind goes, energy flows. The greater the FREQUENCY of thought, the more energy will be directed towards whatever you place your attention upon. The higher the frequency, the greater the vibration. Imagine the energy that creates an earthquake. The earth has massive amounts of energy that is constantly in vibration. When that energy is concentrated (much like in your mind) at a higher frequency, it can literally move mountains. You can move mountains within your own life if you can maintain your focus enough to shift your energy.

Do you consistently experience high-level emotions OR are you constantly vibrating from low-level emotions?

Your "vibe rate" and the frequency of high or low-level emotions associated with that frequency will determine the quality of your reality and your happiness. Remember, from the quantum model of thinking, it's not bad to be sad or angry. If someone cuts you off while driving, you may get angry for a moment, but your ability to go back to a calm level of homeostasis is a good indicator of how you're "vibing" and the ability to move freely through your emotions.

Real emotional intelligence is not just about doing the meditations and breathwork. It's about your ability to respond when you face high levels of stress and maintain your focus. Chronic unhappiness, depression, and anxiety really comes down to being aware of your emotions and where they are coming from.

The real question is, "How are you managing your (e-motional) energy to vibrate at a higher frequency?"

It's not about what happens to you. It's about whether you respond or react to what happens to you. Imagine being a drop of water, sending out ripples that affect the lives of everybody around you. Whether you emit positive or negative emotions it really comes down to your awareness and that is emotional mastery. The opposite is when other people, the external world - things that you have no control over are like ripples…maybe even tidal waves, washing over you, and taking you completely off-course. This is a place where a simple shift in our awareness from "Why is this happening to me to what can I learn from this experience and be grateful for?"

Breathwork, Brain Waves, and Emotions

We've discussed this briefly in Chapter 1, but now we are going deeper into the science of *breathwork* and how it affects brainwaves, emotions, and the nervous system. If you've been doing your homework and getting in your regular breathwork, you will begin to notice physiological adaptations within the body in terms of your ability to manage stress. Consistent breathwork creates an inner calming that connects the nervous system to the brain and body in new ways. This is where we can create new neural pathways by calming ourselves down into theta brain wave state. It is in this state that we can reprogram the subconscious mind.

The subconscious mind ONLY works on images. Your conscious mind is paying attention to everything happening in front of you right now, reading these words. The subconscious mind has no awareness of positive or negative and is purely focused on images. Then we have the unconscious mind where things are abstract in the form of blobs or shapes.

As we progress through the shadow awakening process, things may still rise up from the unconscious, through our subconscious, producing images that can provide us guidance or clues to when and where we are still shedding or have yet to integrate layers of our shadow.

Consistent meditation or breathwork and calming the nervous system helps soften up the logical mind and can allow us to access our emotions and break down unconscious blockages limiting access to the shadow or repressed emotions. This softening can make it easier to access trauma, integrate the shadow, allow stuck emotions to move through the body, heal from lingering pain, and even generational wounds.

Brain Waves

Here we are going to focus on five different brain waves. With meditation and breathwork practice, you can shift your brainwave state through these different levels in the same way that you would shift through the gears of a car.

Do you need to get a bunch of busy work done? You'll need to be in a *beta* brainwave state. Do you need to relax and let some creative ideas come your way? Then you should relax a little into the alpha brainwave state to calm the mind chatter. What if you want to start reprogramming your subconscious mind? Then allow yourself to fall deeply into theta brainwave "flow state." If it's time to go to sleep and get some quality rest, then let's close our eyes and go into delta brainwaves. Gamma brainwaves are levels of deep bliss like a Buddhist monk and are only accessed in deep states of meditation.

Knowing the science behind how your brain works, and how your emotions function, allows you to become like a superhero - with the power to manage your own energy and e-motions.

You can work with different brainwaves, by utilizing the breathwork and meditation exercises included with this book or the video course. The key to incorporating these exercises is to shift your conscious awareness and access these different states to create the calm space in your mind, specifically your nervous system to shift any stuck or blocked emotions in your body. Transmutation can only occur when you calm down your mind and body. It's difficult to tap into your body to release emotions when thoughts are spinning around in your head space. Don't feel discouraged if this doesn't work the first time. It may take multiple sessions of meditation or breathwork to disconnect from your mind and tap into your body.

Make sure to utilize your journal and note what comes up in this space when doing your inner work practice. A big part of doing this work is tapping into any residual emotional energy that may still be lurking deeper in the shadow space. Sometimes we are working with one emotion but it's really a distraction from something deeper that we did not see when we first started doing this work. For example, let's say we are working with our anger, and as we go deeper into our anger, we discover that emotion of anger is masking a deeper fear or grief. In the same way that going to the gym strengthens the body, as you build more strength on your path to inner work, your abilities and capacities to move more energy will continue to grow. Remember to be gentle and trust your intuition on this path to inner work. At the end of the day, this journey is all about loving yourself more completely, so enjoy the process. **Make your shadow work journey a labor of love!**

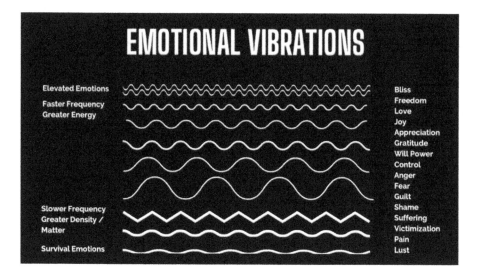

Scale Of Emotions and Energetic Frequencies

When I try to explain this without a graphic…sometimes I sound completely nuts, but with this image it becomes crystal clear that your emotions affect your vibrational energy or "vibe rate." Remember earlier we were talking about vibration and frequency? Here you can see how consistently operating from a low-vibrational emotion literally is slower, denser, and more linear. The more consistently you vibrate at the lower frequency, the denser and more difficult it will appear to be for you to change. But the way things appear has a lot to do with your energy and how you are "vibing" in that moment. The more you direct your energy towards the higher vibrational frequencies, the more momentum you will create to stay oscillating in that higher vibe and this higher frequency will make it easier to break through any barriers that show up.

It will be easier to break through any barriers you have because with your emotions oscillating at a higher frequency you can break through denser material (matter)…especially when things arise from the unconscious mind to be processed and integrated. Imagine this, you are doing shadow work and working with your past traumas. Wouldn't it be easier to break down the dense nature of these experiences if you are emotionally vibrating at a higher level? Remember it's not "good" or "bad" to feel low-vibrational emotions. Emotions let you know when something is not right and it's a place to get curious.

For example, if you approach your shadow from a space of gratitude, appreciation, and bliss when working with guilt or shame, wouldn't it be easy to work with your shame or guilt? Wouldn't your shadow feel safer

Odysseus Andrianos

opening up and healing if you approach it from a different emotional frequency, rather than going in there with anger or attempting to force changes or control it? These are examples and different things work for different people. Another way to look at this technique is like jump-starting a vehicle by electrifying a low-vibe frequency with a higher-vibe frequency to get the engine going again.

We discussed how people could literally get hormonally addicted to a low-vibrational frequency and not even be aware they are doing this from a shadow perspective. But throughout this book we have taught you how to work with your shadow, manage your emotions, and feel your way into a healing space rather than remaining stuck and just numbing the pain. Now we are going to go deeper into how to recognize your logical reality and the ways that you could be addicted to a cycle of sabotage.

Another way of understanding the difference in these frequencies comes back to the first chapter of this book. If you look at the lower-vibrational frequencies, they are more linear while the higher-vibrational frequencies are more wave-like. This is scientific evidence of what we've been expressing since the beginning of this book. The lower vibrational emotions are denser and represent the Newtonian, 3D, particle-based reality. The denser the emotions and the lower the vibration, the more stuck you become in that frequency. But this is precisely where the content in this chapter explains how, through our awareness, we can transmute and polarize those emotions and operate at a higher frequency which really is you performing at the *quantum* level of consciousness.

Let's simplify this: Do you really think you're going to have an easy time creating or manifesting your dreams when you're operating from a space of fear, anger, guilt, shame, sadness, and victimhood? I'll be honest and say that anger and fear can allow you to get some things accomplished in the short term because you'll be pumping out lots of adrenaline. But this is what leads to chronic burnout of your kidneys and adrenal glands because you're constantly in "fight or flight" mode. This is actually where much of society is today, causing extreme stress and chronic disease because our nervous systems have been hardwired into this place of the sympathetic system and adrenal burnout.

In the long term, we will consistently get more done, feel safer and calmer in our experience, and can heal more efficiently when our bodies are operating from a higher vibrational frequency of love, gratitude, appreciation, and bliss. When we do the work mentioned in this book to calm our nervous system down and vibrate at a higher frequency, we can neurologically rewire our minds and bodies to operate from this state. This is where real healing occurs. A healthy nervous system should be able to move from "fight or flight" mode to "rest and recovery" mode with ease, but this is not how most people's bodies operate because of the extreme stress placed on the average person in society today.

Rewiring The Mind

When it comes to the nervous system and changing our reality, we have to understand how the electrical network of our neurology functions. Once we know how it operates, we can begin to change the wiring to create the desired result we choose.

First, let's begin to explain how the neurologic system works when we have an addiction to food, or abusive relationships, or gambling…Here's how it works:

Trigger>>>> **Meaning**>>>> **Emotion**>>>>**Behavior**

What many people do…they commonly skip the meaning part. They get triggered and go right to the emotion which leads to the behavior. Before assessing the emotion or the behavior, ask yourself, "Why did I do it? What is the meaning?"

(Your shadow is likely hiding here.)

To correct self-sabotage and self-destruction, we think it is the behavior we need to change…but this is NOT true. Changing behaviors is the end result. Most people only look at the "effects" of their actions, without getting clear on what the "causes" REALLY are. What is the *meaning* that is creating the *emotion* and resulting in the SAME *behavioral* cycles?

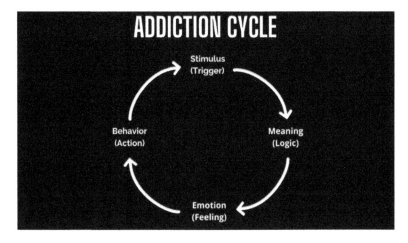

Odysseus Andrianos

To create lasting change, we must become highly aware of our triggers and the stimulus that is creating the trigger. From there we can *get curious* as to what meaning we are creating from that stimulus. The meaning we create is what releases a hormonal response based upon the emotion we feel within the body…which then leads to our habitual behaviors.

A great way of expressing this is cyclical; you're either spiraling upwards or downwards. Many people have not worked with their shadow, their emotions, or let go of their past trauma, and they are completely spiraling out of control with their lives. They may have become hormonally and neurologically addicted to low-vibe emotions and are probably completely unaware that their shadow is running their lives. It may sound crazy to some, but many of us have had an "aha" moment in our lives where we woke up one day and said, "Why am I still doing this or living like this?"

Possibly the greatest GOLD nugget from doing this inner work with your emotions is that as you integrate your shadow, you'll eventually be able to see when others are projecting their shadow onto you, and you'll become less triggered by them. An important point to understand is that even after doing this work, you'll still trigger others and may get triggered yourself, but you won't be as susceptible to falling back into old behaviors because you've done the work to heal your emotional wounds. Remain patient when communicating with others and always stay grounded.

A key point to realize here is that not everyone in your life is going to work on themselves. Your emotionally wounded father, mother, auntie, sibling, uncle or friend…it's highly possible they're just not going to do this inner work for various reasons. But, we cannot judge them for that. The best thing we can do is be compassionate toward them, and by doing this work on ourselves it will be easier to manage what's coming up for them without it affecting us or at least having less of an effect upon us. Remember, it all comes down to energy. Our ability to manage our energy is crucial to our well-being, which we will go over more in the Boundaries section of Chapter 7.

Section Review

- Emotional Mastery means being "tuned in" to your body, mind, and nervous system. Be able to polarize your emotions and don't get out of balance when highly triggered.

- Mastery means using your emotions instead of letting your emotions use you. Someone who's out of touch with their emotions is likely to get stuck in "fight or flight" mode or run a program based on emotional reactions from their limbic system when their amygdala gets activated.

- Understanding how to polarize your emotions means being aware of the opposing emotion you are feeling and being able to feel your way into that opposing emotion, even when triggered. Instead of feeling fear, you can choose to find faith in a situation.

- Be crystal clear on how the Triune brain functions, and be aware of where your brain is operating from and where others are operating from as well. Know when to engage and when to back off based on how you're feeling and assessing others emotional energy.

- Our entire universe is made up of vibration and frequency. When we become aware of our emotions, we become aware of our vibrational frequency. We can have low-vibes and high-vibes. We can fine-tune this energy as we master our emotions.

- Consistently use breathwork, together with the function of different brainwaves, to shift your nervous system, vibrational frequency, and emotions.

- Get familiar with the five different brainwaves: Beta, Alpha, Theta, Delta, and Gamma. Be aware of which vibrational frequency you are working from to master your nervous system.

- Apply the scale of emotions as a map to measure whether you are in a slow or low-vibrational frequency or in a high-vibrational frequency - 3D vs. Quantum.

- Rewire the brain by becoming aware of the meaning you are creating when triggered. Trigger > Meaning > Emotion > Behavior. Change the *meaning* to shift your *emotions*, if you want to change the *behavior*.

Section 2: Law Of Polarity: Emotional Mastery

Chronic low-level emotions can lead to disease within the body and can even become addicting. The goal of emotional polarity is to use your emotions instead of letting them use you. We've already begun working with the emotions and here we want to identify how to polarize them.

List any emotions you're still working with and what the opposing emotions are:

Emotion   **Opposite Emotion**

_____   _____

_____   _____

_____   _____

_____   _____

How often do you find yourself stuck in old emotions and what behaviors are still consistently showing up for you? Remember that when your **amygdala** is triggered, you cannot see the long-term of an emotional situation.

_____

_____

_____

_____

Brain Waves

Are you clear on brainwaves and what type of activities you would be engaging in when accessing different brainwave states? Please list below to make sure you understand:

Beta- _____

Alpha- _____

Theta- _____

Delta- _____

Gamma- _____

Emotional Vibrations

Denser and slower vibration keep you stuck in the 3D model. Less dense wave-like high-vibe emotions keep you operating from the quantum level of consciousness.

List three low-vibe emotions and three high-vibe emotions:

<u>Low Vibe</u>	<u>High Vibe</u>
(Dense/Linear) Emotions	(Less Dense/Quantum) Emotions
_____	_____
_____	_____
_____	_____
_____	_____

Rewiring The Mind

Our low-vibrational emotions keep us stuck in the 3D Linear model of consciousness. It's becoming aware of our triggers that allows us to change the meaning that shifts the emotion, which changes our behaviors so we can operate from the Quantum Wave model of reality.

Are there any triggers still showing up for you, what are they?

_____

_____

_____

_____

When meaning are you still using to keep you stuck in 3D when triggered and what new meaning could you create from your triggers? (Meaning can often be the limiting beliefs.)

Old Meaning

New Meaning

_____   _____

_____   _____

_____   _____

_____   _____

_____   _____

_____   _____

_____   _____

_____   _____

HOMEWORK

(Schedule some time each day for your inner work practice)

1. Are there any triggers still consistently showing up in your life? Make sure to identify them so you can shift the meaning you are creating.

_____

_____

_____

_____

2. Which emotions are still repressed causing you to show up inauthentically and sabotage your life?

_____

_____

_____

_____

3. When you look at your past, are there any consistent low-vibrational frequency emotions that have been holding you back?

_____

_____

_____

_____

4. Make sure to keep up with your breathwork and meditation practice, mantras, and making physical and mental health a priority in your life.

_____

_____

_____

_____

Odysseus Andrianos

Questions to answer before the next section of the book:

Have you gotten clear on areas where your shadow could still be running the show?

_____

_____

_____

_____

Are there any recurring thoughts that are still showing up to sabotage you?

_____

_____

_____

_____

Is there anything you could still be clinging to emotionally that's not allowing you the space energetically to receive what you deserve?

_____

_____

_____

_____

"You are not thinking. You are merely being logical."

— Niels Bohr

CHAPTER SIX

Section 1: Logical Fallacies: Recognize Illogical Thinking

What are Logical Fallacies?

A *fallacy* is a false notion or a mistaken belief. A *logical fallacy* is when incorrect information or faulty logic is used as evidence to support an argument. The word "fallacy" has its roots in the Latin word *fallacia,* meaning: "**to lie or deceive.**"

When we learn to identify logical fallacies, it gets easier to spot when they are being used (both *externally* and *internally*). And just like with shadow projection, it's important that we start by looking inward to discover our own fallacies, illogical thoughts, and patterns of thinking. As we gain awareness of our own fallacies, we also become better equipped to recognize any fallacies presented by others whether friends, family, coworkers, or mass media.

This also helps with identifying your shadow or someone else projecting their shadow because our shadow can make us do illogical and irrational things, especially when we're triggered.

Applying the logical fallacies, in conjunction with shadow work and emotional mastery, makes life infinitely easier for you. Not only will it be easier to discern truth, but you will get faster results with less effort because you will not be fooled by faulty arguments or thinking (including your own). Mastering these fallacies is also very beneficial when maintaining boundaries with yourself or with others. You will be equipped with the ability to break down the logical structure of your own thoughts or someone else's argument(s) while maintaining your boundaries with your new rhetorical skills.

There are hundreds of logical fallacies. In the scope of this book, we will go over the most valuable, pertinent, and useful ones for today's modern society. But we hope you will do your own research and practice these on your own to master their meaning.

Language Arts

Language arts are much like a martial arts practice...words are like (s)words. You create your reality with them, cutting through the air like a sword, manifesting your consciousness with each paragraph. A "paragraph" is like a parallel-graph between your mind and the external world. When we master the basics of language arts, especially logical thinking, we become master creators of our reality.

Another way of looking at this is to stop cutting yourself with (s)words or sabotaging yourself with your limiting beliefs and giving in to your inner critic. Having a faulty language structure can lead to less favorable results in every aspect of life. The results won't change until we cultivate the awareness to recognize what we are creating from the unconscious (especially if our shadow has been running the show).

One of my favorite examples of faulty language structure, and not being aware of your thinking, is using the word "try." When you "try" to do things, it leaves so much space for you to fail and say, "Well, I tried." Instead of saying "I tried," don't be afraid to be honest and say "I failed," and begin examining when and where you failed. Remember, from a *quantum* level nothing is either "good" or "bad." Our ego can fear accepting failure, but this is a sign of not accepting your potential and protecting yourself from seeing where you need to grow or blossom.

It is also important to be clear about our intent when we set out to do things. Saying "I'm going to try" is different from saying, "I am going to do my best." Committing to doing your best completely changes the energy around our approach to whatever it is we want to accomplish. Even Jedi master Yoda said, "Do or do not, there is no try."

If our language structure is faulty, and we do not know how to assess our thoughts properly, we can easily fall prey to ourselves or our unconscious beliefs. Often this is where our repetitive thoughts are keeping us stuck because we could still be operating from a linear (Newtonian) 3D model of consciousness. If you're consistently, unconsciously creating your reality from a place of deeply limiting beliefs, you will be living a limited life.

Recall from Chapter 2 the beliefs that arise from our shadow self, such as: "I'm not worthy of love," "My feelings aren't valid," and "I'm not good enough." These faulty language patterns that we can unconsciously be addicted to can run our lives and keep us from living a fulfilling life. This is why our consistent meditation, breathwork, and journaling practices are keys to sustained success on the journey to healing our emotional pain. These low-vibe emotions can be highly addicting, and if we are not conscious of how they are creating our reality, then we can sabotage ourselves. This is exceedingly important when examining our own language structure or language arts.

The first key to success is recognizing how we are sabotaging ourselves. As we progress in our ability to recognize the logical fallacies we are using to create our reality, we will soon be able to see it in others. In fact, it becomes quite fascinating how you'll develop what could be equated to a super power in your ability to see others creating their lives with faulty thinking or reasoning.

Faulty language structure is often the product of a society that perpetuates illogical or "unconscious" thinking. It's easier to sell products to people in a completely unconscious state of awareness. Good marketing and sales are not about teaching you HOW to think for yourself: it's about telling you WHAT to think so you'll buy their product. This is why learning how to think logically, and discern truth from fallacy, is like a super power especially when used in conjunction with the newly found emotional mastery skills you've acquired from this book. This power is equivalent to having an alchemized mind balanced *logical analysis tempered intuitive, and emotional intelligence.* Someone with an integrated shadow who can think for themselves is a high-functioning adult who is truly the master of their reality.

How to Assess Logic

Logic is a language that must be learned. It builds upon a foundation of grammar. Before we can arrive at a logical decision, we must assess the WHO, WHAT, WHEN, and WHERE of the situation. These are the building blocks in a house (or sentence) made of words. The pieces that make up the house are the grammar. As we build the house, we develop a better *understanding* of how the pieces fit together and their relationship to one another. This is the foundation of logical thinking, fundamental to proper awareness and discernment of truth.

Logic helps us figure out the WHY, but if we don't develop a solid understanding of the grammar first, then the "why" we arrive at might not be logical at all. If crucial pieces, the pieces that make a solid foundation of understanding of a house are missing, would you want to live there? Just as you wouldn't want to stand under a structure supported by a weak foundation, you don't want to blindly accept information as truth without the grammar to back it up. Logical thinking is UNDER-STANDING. If it's not logical, it may be a fallacy that could come crashing down on top of you.

Triune Brain Review

Do you remember the *Triune Brain* model from the Quantum Thinking section of Chapter 1? Well, it's crucial here to know that thinking logically when the amygdala has been triggered is nearly impossible. At that point, we're operating from the emotional "limbic" brain and it becomes very hard to recognize these logical fallacies. Could you imagine trying to solve a math problem while being chased by a tiger? When we're emotionally triggered into "fight or flight" mode, our critical thinking and reason go out the window so the brain can focus on basic survival.

Being highly emotional blocks our ability to properly assess and make logical decisions. But with practice, we can recognize the signs pointing to which part of the brain is currently dominant. And once we have this awareness, it becomes possible to bring ourselves back to a space where we can use these tools effectively to create better outcomes even in the heat of the moment. We needed to touch on that again briefly before we dive into the fallacies as a reminder that we need to be in a calm state of mind to properly assess logical thinking.

Following is a brief list of some fallacies and examples to help identify and avoid them in your life. (*There are hundreds of different fallacies to watch out for. These are some of the more common ones.*)

The Logical Fallacies

Appeal to Emotion - Using emotional manipulation (fear, flattery, guilt, sympathy, anger, etc.) to overwhelm reason. (*This one is BIG to watch out for in our own mind chatter.*)

Example:

If I don't eat this last piece of cake, it will go to waste, and Grandma will be sad. I don't want to make her sad.

Appeal to Ignorance - Arguing that because something hasn't been proven true, it must be false or because something hasn't been proven false, it must be true.

Example:

My coworker never compliments me on my looks. That proves they find me unattractive.

Ad Hominem - Attacking a person's character instead of addressing their argument.

(Remember: *Don't shoot the messenger!*)

Example:

Person #1: So many people are suffering from mental health problems these days. We should produce more drugs to keep people numbed to their emotional pain.

Person #2: Prescription drugs can help some people, but I've been having amazing success improving my mental state by working on integrating my shadow and healing my emotions.

Person #1: Sorry, but most people are idiots and idiots can't heal their emotions. If you really believe that would work, then you must be an idiot, too.

Appeal to Popularity (Bandwagon Fallacy) - Pointing to the fact that many people are doing something as evidence that it is the right thing to do.

Example:

Person #1: Have a shot of this top-shelf tequila. Everyone loves this stuff!

Person #2: Thanks, but I'm on a diet right now and being conscious about what I put in my body.

Person #1: Yeah. I know you're on a diet right now. But we've been taking shots for hours, so even if you take a double right now to catch up, you'll still be drinking way less than everyone else. That's "diet" right?

Slippery Slope - Arguing that one action or choice (cause) will cascade into a series of results (effects), ending with an undesirable outcome.

Example:

If you start working out, your muscles will get huge, everyone will be intimidated by you. You'll get so big that all your clothes will rip and you'll scare away all your friends. If you don't want to live at the gym and wear rags, then you better keep away from the gym.

Appeal to Tradition (Argument from Antiquity) - Saying that because something has a long history, it must be the right thing to do.

Example:

The men in our family have always been the strong silent type. We don't show our emotions to other people. They stay locked away deep inside. I don't "feel" things. That's what's best.

Red Herring - Attempting to change the subject and redirect the argument in a different direction.

Example:

Person #1: I've never felt better since I started exercising, eating healthy, and working to integrate my repressed emotions. Do you want to join me?

Person #2: Being healthy is cool. But I feel good when eating ice cream and watching some Netflix. Have you seen the latest episode of "Ice Cream Fantasy?"

Straw Man Fallacy - Misrepresenting the other side to make their argument appear weaker and easier to attack.

Example:

Person #1: Don't you feel great when exercising and eating healthy?

Person #2: You know…I think people can find other ways to feel good besides spending too many hours in the gym every day and eating nothing but kale smoothies.

False Dichotomy - Arguing that it's either/or because there are only two possible choices.

Example:

Person #1: You're either a Coke drinker or a Pepsi drinker. Which one do you prefer?

Person #2: I choose neither. I create my own path of exercise, eating healthy, healing my body, integrating my shadow, and striving to become the best version of myself.

Hasty Generalization - Drawing overly broad conclusions using inadequate evidence.

Example:

Two of my friends lost weight even though they kept drinking alcohol and eating whatever they wanted. That proves alcohol and food choices have no impact on weight loss.

Slothful Induction Fallacy (Appeal to Coincidence) - A reasonable argument is dismissed as coincidence despite strong supporting evidence. (Opposite of Hasty Generalization.)

Example:

Person #1: Sally has been exercising and eating healthy for years. She looks and feels great.

Person #2: Yeah, that's because Sally has such great genes. It's not what she's been doing, she's just lucky and I'm not.

Appeal to Authority - Using a position of authority as evidence that the argument is correct.

Example:

Person #1: My doctor says I can eliminate my restless leg syndrome with medication, and that diet and exercise are not necessary.

Person #2: But won't diet and exercise have better side effects?

Person #1: I don't know. He's my doctor, so I do whatever he says.

Circular Reasoning - When you attempt to make an argument by beginning with an assumption that you are trying to prove is already true.

Example:

Using logic is important because it's important to use logic.

Logical Truths

Keep in mind that someone's argument could be completely truthful, and completely lacking logic. A perfect example is an *appeal to emotion* fallacy. Someone is directly attempting to activate your limbic brain so you'll make an emotional decision. *"You would look and feel better if you were driving this new car."* It may be true that you would look great driving that new car, but that argument is not a logical reason to make the purchase. Many of us encounter these fallacies regularly. (We may even use them ourselves or have been using them without knowing it.) Now that you can bring these fallacies to your awareness, it will be much easier for you to identify where they come up and to not let them lead you astray.

Section Review

- The word *fallacy* means "false notion or mistaken belief." We examine language structure to find logically fallacious arguments hidden within seemingly truthful statements.

- Use the tools of shadow work, emotional mastery, and the logical fallacies to eliminate false beliefs and maintain your boundaries as you build a greater connection with your shadow.

- There are hundreds of logical fallacies. We introduced 13 of them in the scope of this book to get you familiar with some of the more common ones.

- Language arts are like martial arts, and words are like (s)words. Mastering our language structure helps us to recognize where our inner critic or shadow is showing up to sabotage us.

- Eliminate the word "try" from your life. As Master Yoda said, "Do, or do not."

- Grammar represents the building blocks of logical understanding. We will not be able to arrive at WHY to make a logical decision if we don't first know the Who, What, When, and Where.

- Remember to *check yourself* and use the Triune Brain as a map to assess where your mind is operating from. Are you in your Neocortex, Limbic, or Reptilian brain?

- Go over the fallacies in this book multiple times to become a language arts master. Study more fallacies on your own and add them to your repertoire to become a word ninja.

Section 2: Recognizing Illogical Thinking: Logical Fallacies

This section is a little different than the other sections, but arguably the most important to understand how your logical mind works. We will go through a range of fallacies and make sure you have a decent grasp on them. It's not always easy to remember these, but the more repetition the better, so be patient with yourself and practice them regularly.

A fallacy is a false notion or mistaken belief.

Learning to identify logical fallacies will allow you to discern truth more easily from fiction, which will help you think more logically and be less likely to fall into the emotional trap of the limbic system). This is especially important when people present **"false"** information and try to manipulate you with emotionally triggering comments. It's also crucial to discover where your own shadow's limiting beliefs could still be manipulating you.

Language Arts

The language arts are like martial arts, but instead of karate-chopping some wood, we use words like (s)words to penetrate the mind. It's essential first to make sure that we are not cutting ourselves with these words or swords. Our internal dialogue is where the inner critic or shadow could still be feeding you fallacies and unconsciously sabotaging your life.

How to Assess Logic

Logic is like a house built upon a solid foundation of under-standing. A solid foundation is especially important when it comes to the thoughts and beliefs inside our own mind. Before making a logical decision (or standing under the house), we must make sure our grammar is rock solid and not riddled with holes or made of shoddy materials (fallacies).

What are the four pillars of building the house? (Hint: They lead you to "WHY.")

_____

_____

_____

The Logical Fallacies

Write down the definition or an example of each logical fallacy and do your best to relate it to your own life. This work might take a little longer than the other sections, but it will be so worth it because doing the exercise will help the concepts stick in your mind. Feel free to use the Internet to look up the definitions to help you answer these. It took me months before I mastered them, so take your time. Your understanding of these fallacies will improve your ability to communicate and argue effectively in the future.

Appeal to Emotion -

_____

Appeal to Ignorance -

_____

Ad Hominem -

_____

Appeal to Popularity (Bandwagon) -

_____

Slippery Slope -

_____

Appeal to Tradition (Argument From Antiquity) -

_____

Red Herring -

_____

Straw Man -

_____

False Dichotomy -

Hasty Generalization -

Slothful Induction Fallacy (Appeal to Coincidence) -

Appeal to Authority -

Circular Reasoning -

Logical Truths

Keep in mind that someone's argument could be completely truthful, and also completely lacking logic. Awakening NEO and staying primarily in your logical neocortex will help you protect your own best interest, especially when it comes to your **boundaries**. The *Appeal to Emotion* is a perfect example of how another person or your own shadow could use your emotions to keep you stuck in the Matrix of old ways of thinking and limiting your potential.

There are hundreds of logical fallacies. We only go over 13 in this course to keep it simple for you, but please get curious, keep digging, and studying more to develop your skill set.

HOMEWORK

(Schedule some time each day for your inner work practice)

1. Which logical fallacies do you see most often in your life?

_____

_____

_____

_____

2. In what areas of your life could your shadow still manipulate you with illogical thinking?

_____

_____

_____

_____

3. Do any of these fallacies stand out in your life or trigger you?

_____

_____

_____

_____

4. Make sure to keep up with your breathwork and meditation practice, mantras, and making physical and mental health a priority in your life.

_____

_____

_____

_____

Questions to answer before the next section of the book:

Do you struggle with boundaries in any area of your life?

_____

_____

_____

_____

Do you have difficulty speaking your truth or easily sharing it with others?

_____

_____

_____

_____

Is it challenging for you to be open and receive things from others or get what you want?

_____

_____

_____

_____

Who could you be if you had stronger boundaries and were crystal clear on your intentions?

_____

_____

_____

_____

If you could attract anything into your life right now, what would it be?

_____

_____

_____

_____

"The only people who get upset about you setting boundaries are the ones who were benefiting from you having none."

—Unknown

CHAPTER SEVEN

Section 1: Boundaries: The Law of Gender

What are Boundaries, and Why are they so Important?

Let's begin by saying this chapter is arguably the most critical section of this book. Understanding the *Law of Gender* how to effectively establish boundaries and maintain them can literally shift peoples' entire lives. Throughout this chapter we begin to get really clear on who we are, what really serves our higher purpose, and what boundaries need to be clearly established to allow our disease to manifest instead of trying to control or force things to happen.

Boundaries are essential to maintaining a healthy lifestyle. They allow you to maintain focus and not get distracted or overindulge in actions or people that do not serve your higher purpose or goals. Many people have lived their lives without boundaries and this is precisely why their lives are falling apart or why they do not feel satisfied where they are. When we have clear boundaries, we can use the *Law of Gender* to recognize where we are out of balance in our masculine or feminine (yang or yin) nature. We can also recognize when others are out of balance or violating our boundaries. This knowledge is a game-changer when it comes to long-term mental, and emotional health.

What is the Law of Gender?

Gender is in everything. All things have both a male and female principle. Masculine is the giver, and the feminine is the receiver. When we combine both effectively, we become a master at creating our world and creating our reality. This symbol would be the line running between the yin and yang, known as the middle way path. When we live a balanced life, we will quickly see whether we are effectively maintaining our boundaries or letting our shadow run the show.

Boundary Basics

Boundaries are crucial to your personal identity; and your mental, physical, and emotional health. You need to be clear with yourself when things don't "feel right." This is how your shadow shows up after you've integrated it. Your boundaries turn the triggers of fear and anxiety into your guide. Instead of your shadow sabotaging you and your behaviors, it becomes your ally. Now that you listen more deeply to your shadow, what's really triggering you will actually show you which people, places, and things you need to establish new boundaries with or, in some cases, completely cut out of your life. (This is entirely up to you to decide based on your connection and feelings.)

By establishing proper boundaries, it will be easier to recognize your shadow and show up more authentically as your higher self - guiding you rather than your shadow or lower self-sabotaging you. This is why we go over shadow work before discussing boundaries, because working with the shadow eventually gives you clues into the real things that are affecting you and what needs to be shifted now in your current reality. With this awareness, instead of fighting your emotions, you are in tune with them and know what is not vibrating at your frequency. By cultivating this connection with your emotions, you'll be more available to receive the love you deserve.

5 Types of Boundaries

Mental - Freedom of thinking, beliefs, values, etc.

"Respecting others' opinions and not forcing your own."

Emotional - Dismissing emotions and/or dumping them.

"Not discussing topics that make you or others uncomfortable."

Physical - Inappropriate touching or sexual comments.

"Be clear what is acceptable and appropriate for you."

Material - Possessions, when they can be used and how.

"Let others know what is acceptable and what is not."

Time/Energy - People being late and not respectful of your time.

"If people are going to be late then they should let you know."

A Sacred Practice

Setting boundaries is the foundation of your mental health, and should be considered a sacred practice. When we set our boundaries, whether they are for ourselves or with other people, we need consistent rituals each day that help us maintain our path to fulfilling the commitment to our inner work.

This can be a challenge when introducing new boundaries to people who have crossed them or hurt you in the past. The best way to do this is to begin with the outcome in mind. Maybe your long-term goal is to get someone out of your life, but for now you still have to work or live with them. Let's say it's a roommate, family member, or a coworker who you have consistent close contact with, but you want to establish stronger boundaries.

The best way to begin is to make note of all the triggers or things about this person that set you off and put you out of balance. By listing these things, you're creating more awareness around them, so you can know how to manage them more effectively when they come up. Suppose people you are working with have consistent behaviors that trigger you. In that case you can plan ahead to possibly redirect them into a new action or way of being that makes the situation more comfortable for you. This can make communicating your boundaries easier for them to adapt to and integrate into their daily routine.

Keep in mind, if you are not clear about your desired intention, then it is likely you will not receive it. So, if necessary, write your intentions down and remember that your boundaries are sacred. It's important to honor your beliefs, stand up for what you're willing to tolerate, and be firm in protecting your emotions when you feel uncomfortable. Feeling your emotions is not a "good" or "bad" thing, and is often just a signal something is not right or needs to shift. As we get more into the Law of Gender, it will be easier to identify imbalances and incongruencies in your thoughts and when others are attempting to break down your boundaries to manipulate or control you.

Boundary Examples

You may have a strong emotion towards someone or something and get attached to a certain outcome. This attachment to the outcome can cause you to show up inauthentically because you were so attached to the outcome or how you thought you wanted things to be that you missed out on what was happening right in front of you.

This is what happens when our minds get caught up in that 3D model and we spoil our future based upon our past. If this occurs consistently, we can recognize this as a trigger pointing to where we may not have fully processed a past trauma or integrated a repressed or suppressed emotion. This causes anxiety or attachment to an outcome which ruins our ability to be in the moment and fully present with our energy. This is an area where lacking internal boundaries can show up as a breakdown in our external relationships, or failing to bring our ideas to fruition. (This can also be a mirror into areas where we need to work on our relationship with ourselves and our own attachments based upon past experiences.)

Setting and maintaining proper boundaries makes it easier to not be attached to an outcome, while still being clear about the path you are taking towards achieving a desired result. If you choose to be attached to anything, be attached to the service of others, because as you will see with the Law of Gender, energy moves based on how you receive it and how you let it go. If you are in service to others, it will always come back to you so there is no need to be attached to an outcome. The ability to surrender is a feminine trait and is the essence of a quantum mind. When we surrender, it renders our reality to allow limitless possibilities to arise.

Boundaries and Gender

Many people get out of balance in their lives, and they are completely unaware they are doing it from a shadow perspective. But when it comes to boundaries, understanding the principles of gender can be a game changer in terms of manifesting your desires and living the life you deserve. In this section, we will go over a variety of ways that will help you to differentiate between your masculine and feminine energies. Keep in mind this has NOTHING to do with sex or being male or female. The idea is all based on ancient principles of gender (Yin & Yang) and how our external and internal worlds are created based upon balancing these energies.

Here is a common example where both men and women can get out of balance with their masculinity: Many people these days especially business owners and mothers can get too much into their masculine or Yang energy because they have to constantly be "in control" of everything externally. When we are constantly controlling things externally, this does not allow the space energetically to receive internally. Being in touch with our feminine side allows us to receive.

Excessive yang energy can also create hormonal imbalances. This could create a neurological addiction to "fight or flight" mode where our bodies and minds become so unconsciously addicted to controlling everything that we begin to feel awkward or uncomfortable allowing ourselves to receive or surrender to our "Yin" feminine nature. This happens to both men and women. This may stem back to childhood traumas, repressed emotions, and limiting beliefs like "I'm not worthy of love," or "I'm not good enough." This unconscious projection keeps everything external, NOT allowing us to feel and embrace our feminine Yin side, and keeps our hearts from opening and feeling worthy of receiving the love we need and deserve.

Constantly being in our Yang masculine energy, which is the way much of society operates, causes us to burn out, lack empathy, and not create the space for us to relax or surrender to the love we deserve. We have been using breathwork and meditation techniques to help rewire the mind, calm it down, and activate the parasympathetic nervous system from the beginning of this book. In this space, our bodies are relaxed and calm enough to enter rest and recovery mode, where we can do deeper healing. Knowing how the body and nervous system work also translates into awareness of how the Law of Gender works. This knowledge leads to recognizing where we have gotten out of balance both internally and externally. By tuning into our bodies, and our hearts, we can listen deeply enough to vibrate at a frequency that creates the life we are worthy of receiving.

Masculinity Traits (Yang)

Right side of the Body and Left side of the Brain

Warm and Active

Excited and Outwardly Directed

Analytical and Rational

Objective and Verbal

Mathematical and Sequential

Highly Logical

You can see that the masculine traits are primarily directed towards what's going on externally. They rationally, and methodically calculate everything using less intuition and more logic.

Feminine Traits (Yin)

Left side of the Body and Right side of the Brain

Cool and Passive

Calming and Inwardly Directed

Holistic and Emotional

Subjective and Non-Verbal

Spatial and Simultaneous

Highly Intuitive

Here we see that the feminine traits are primarily directed towards what's going on internally. Feminine traits include feeling emotions, being calm, aware, and in tune with our hearts using less logic and more intuition.

Out of Balance Masculinity

Aggressive or Abusive

Controlling

Confrontational

Overly Competitive

Unstable or Withdrawn

Unsupportive

Here we see the out of balance masculine being so outwardly directed that it tries to control and dominate others, and is unavailable to support others' ideas. In an overly masculine state, we are unavailable to receive and may establish boundaries that block us from receiving love. Is this showing up in your life, or are there people in your life who are out of balance?

Out of Balance Feminine

Extreme Emotions

Demanding

Excessive Neediness

Manipulative/Inauthentic

People Pleasing

Victim/Insecurity

Here we see the out of balance feminine being so inwardly directed those emotions are taken to the extreme. In an overly feminine state, we may become manipulative toward others and become inauthentic in order to please others. Self-sacrifice can cause us to feel stuck in victimhood, and not establish any boundaries so we cannot be clear about the love we deserve. Is this showing up in your life or are people in your life who are out of balance?

Identifying Healthy Boundaries

Below are examples where your boundaries, or those of people around you, could be out of balance. Keep an eye out for these as red flags and make sure you stick to your path and not allow others to interfere.

Financial - Sticking to a budget and focusing on long term goals.

Mental - Limiting screen time (phone, tv, iPad).

Psychological - Negative self-talk or talking about others.

Physical - Maintaining a regular sleep and workout schedule.

Relationships - Avoiding people and thoughts that suck energy from you.

Diet - Eliminating unhealthy food, thoughts, and people from our fridge, minds, and lives.

Emotional - Allowing ourselves to feel and process repressed emotions.

Could you be imbalanced in your masculine or feminine nature in any of these areas?

A final key point here is the realization of what's known as the *Middle Way Path* in Eastern philosophy. When we've fully integrated our shadow, and are now walking the awakened shadow path, we have essentially balanced out our Yin and Yang (or masculine or feminine) nature. Being masculine or feminine is not bad or good. It's the imbalance that causes disharmony in one's life. This point comes back to the starting point of this course: **"Awareness."** Instead of dealing with the effects in our lives, we become the "cause" due to our acute awareness. This awareness is what sets us free from the shackles of our knowable linear past which we discussed in chapter one.

A properly integrated shadow is essentially a balanced Yin and Yang nature of the mind. We could even say it's an alchemized mind, as the body, mind, and heart work in harmony with our highest self. This is where harmony allows us to truly live a boundless life because of the deeper awareness of things "as they are" rather than perceiving things "as they were." Because we are no longer attached to the wounds of our past, and no longer creating our future unconsciously, we now have the freedom to shift ALL of our relationships. Of course, this shift always begins with our relationship with ourselves first.

Now that we are equipped with the tools to awaken our shadow, we can manifest the life we deserve, and have more fulfilling experiences in all areas of life. Instead of our shadow being an unconscious burden that sabotages us, we have a guide to give us the inspiration and clarity to recognize our triggers. Our weaknesses now become our strengths. Our inner saboteur becomes our ally and we are prepared for future triggers that may occur when deep emotions may arise. But now that we have established a more intimate and complete relationship with ourselves, we can see through our own "stories" or illusions and begin living our lives from a quantum level of infinite abundance on all levels. Thank you for doing this work. We hope you continue to enjoy your journey.

Section Review

- Boundaries are what make it possible to ALLOW your dreams to come true. Instead of fighting yourself to stay on track, you just set the parameters and maintain them.

- Boundaries are essential to maintaining your mental, physical, emotional, and spiritual health.

- Without boundaries, it's challenging to show up authentically. Lacking boundaries is likely a sign of unmanaged inner trauma and/or repressed emotions.

- View establishing boundaries as a sacred practice. Your daily rituals are a means of maintaining your internal and external boundaries.

- Utilize the Law of Gender to recognize where you could be out of balance in your masculine or feminine energy.

- Learn to identify your masculine and feminine energies, and how they can be used effectively in different situations. Also, identify how others use or misuse their masculine and feminine energy to control or manipulate you.

- Being in your masculine or feminine is not "bad" or "good"…but being out of balance in them could show up in pretty ugly ways if we are not aware of how these imbalances could be our shadow running the show.

- Learning to master the balance of masculine and feminine energies within us, allows us to be in a highly creative and adaptable space, where we can harness both our logical and intuitive abilities.

Section 2: The Law of Gender: Boundaries

Gender is in everything. Everything has both masculine and feminine principles. Gender manifests on all planes. Masculine is the giver and feminine is the receiver.

The goal for understanding boundaries and the Law of Gender is a degree of mastering what is known in Buddhism as the "Middle Way" path. It is the line between the Yin and the Yang.

Proper boundaries allow us to live a boundless life, because we set the parameters and do not allow ourselves to get off the path to success.

In what areas of your life are you currently lacking boundaries, and how is this affecting you?

_____

_____

_____

_____

Boundary Basics

Setting boundaries helps us maintain a healthy lifestyle. By recognizing the principles of gender (masculine and feminine energy, we can discover where we, or other people in our life) are crossing the line, limiting us from performing at our best.

What are the five types of boundaries mentioned in the book and which one(s) do you struggle with the most?

1. _____

2. _____

3. _____

4. _____

5. _____

A Sacred Practice

Setting boundaries is the foundation of your mental and emotional health, and should be considered a sacred practice.

What rituals are you performing each day that allow you to access your fullest potential?

_____

_____

_____

_____

Are there any people in your life who you need to establish new boundaries with? Who are they and what boundaries would you like to create?

_____

_____

_____

_____

Creating Boundaries

First, be clear on where you may have lacked boundaries in the past. How has this affected you and how has your attachment to an outcome kept you from being present in the moment in past relationships? Often our lack of boundaries is based upon traumas from our past.

Where in your life could you be showing up inauthentically because you lack boundaries based upon trauma from your past?

_____

_____

_____

_____

Once you are clear on where you lacked boundaries in the past, let's get clarity on your intentions for the future. Like we asked at the start of this course: **What is the future life you deserve?** Proper boundaries will allow it to show up for you.

_____

_____

_____

_____

With proper boundaries in place, an integrated shadow, and awareness of the logical fallacies, what type of future do you "deserve" that you are now allowing into your life?

_____

_____

_____

_____

Masculine & Feminine Polarity

Let's go over masculine and feminine traits and what the _out of balance_ traits look like. You don't need to list all of them, just the one(s) that stand out the most to you.

Masculine Traits	Feminine Traits
_____	_____
_____	_____
_____	_____
_____	_____

Out of Balance Masculine

_____

_____

_____

_____

Out of Balance Feminine

_____

_____

_____

_____

Where could you be out of balance in any of these traits? What do you still need to work on?

_____

_____

_____

_____

Identifying Healthy Boundaries

Circle any that you struggle with or need to work on.

Financial	**Mental**	**Psychological**	**Physical**
Relationships	**Diet**	**Emotional**	

Why do you struggle in these areas? How could you shift them?

_____

_____

_____

_____

HOMEWORK

(Schedule some time each day for your inner work practice.)

1. Identify areas where you may be out of balance in your masculine and feminine energy.

    _____

    _____

    _____

    _____

2. Go over areas of your life where you could be giving or receiving more.

    _____

    _____

    _____

    _____

3. Get clear on your goals and how a breakdown in your boundaries could sabotage you.

    _____

    _____

    _____

    _____

4. Make sure to keep up with your breathwork and meditation practice, mantras, and making physical and mental health a priority in your life.

    _____

    _____

    _____

    _____

Questions to answer before the next section of the course:

Please come up with a list of any questions you may have to complete your shadow awakening journey up to this point in the book before we go over the review section.

_____

_____

_____

_____

Is there anything you are not clear on?

_____

_____

_____

_____

Are there any areas where you feel you still need support?

_____

_____

_____

_____

What are your strengths/weaknesses?

_____

_____

_____

_____

What areas of your life are you still working on?

_____

_____

_____

_____

Are there any deeper emotions or repressed energy within you that still needs to be examined?

_____

_____

_____

_____

If you need any additional support, please email me:
odyandrianos@gmail.com

"Your Shadow is all of the things, 'positive' and 'negative', that you've denied about yourself and hidden beneath the surface of the mask you forgot that you're wearing."

— Oli Anderson

CHAPTER EIGHT

Section 1: Course Review

Welcome to the final section of the course. We hope you've enjoyed the journey and learned much about your human potential through exploring quantum thinking, shadow work, emotional mastery, logical fallacies, and setting stronger boundaries. The end goal of this course is really about helping you on your path to self-actualization and self-realization. We would like to thank you for embarking on this epic odyssey into the abyss of who you are…into the shadow realm and awakening your greatest potential. We hope the tools we've shared have provided you with the fundamentals of knowing not only WHERE to dig, but also HOW to dig into the shadows to find your inner **GOLD**. Remember, **the path is the medicine** and as you heal yourself, your work will heal others, too.

As a final piece, we would like to remind you that everyone is at a different place on their journey to healing, loving themselves, and awakening their shadow. If you felt you needed to go at a slower pace than how we progressed in the course, that's totally okay. If you feel like you're ready to go deeper into the shadow or just simply need more guidance, please let us know. More than anything, we are grateful that you are doing this work because it will not only improve your quality of life, but the lives of everyone around you.In this final section, we will touch briefly on the most important topics from each chapter of the course. If you have any questions that need clarity, or in other words if you get triggered by something here and do not feel clear on anything, please reach out and let us know.

Quantum Thinking

- Recognize how to move from a 3D linear model of "fixed thinking" into a Quantum model of vibrational "infinite thinking."

- Use your awareness to identify triggers, limiting beliefs, your inner critic, self-sabotaging habits, and begin working with your shadow to find your "core conflict."

- Remember the story of the Chinese Farmer: "Are things really "good," or "bad?" Maybe.

- Utilize the model of the Triune Brain as a road map to understand where your mind is operating from. Are you using logic, emotions, or are you in the reptilian brain of "fight" or "flight," mode? Remember to stay out of the matrix of lower brain functions.

- Use breathwork to connect with your shadow, calm the nervous system, and develop a deeper connection to your body as you sift the unconscious mind.

Shadow Work

- Identify what shadow work is. Know how to begin working with repressed emotions, trauma, and energies in the unconscious mind.

- Recognize how and why emotions become stuck in our unconscious and how we can begin accessing this energy to make an internal shift.

- Track your triggers and the meaning you're creating from those triggers. Know what emotions are showing up and how to go deeper into what may be going on below the conscious surface level of the mind.

- Begin working with your shadow and accessing your inner child. Be gentle, compassionate, and more than anything LISTEN to what your shadow's needs are. Often, we need to just sit with our shadow for a bit before any shifts will occur.

- Get curious with your triggers and emotional red flags that pop up. Keep pulling on that thread to get down to your "core conflict" and the emotional energy that is REALLY creating the problem.

Shadow Integration

- Identify the difference between *shadow work* and *shadow integration*. Understand how to access the shadow vs. how to integrate the repressed emotional energy of the shadow.

- Begin integrating the shadow through a range of exercises to calm the nervous system. Relax into "theta" brain wave state, and use mantras to begin working with our subconscious mind and manifest a new reality.

- Not integrating the shadow will affect our lives. Repressed emotions can show up like a "demon" in our lives because at the unconscious level it is just unacknowledged energy.

- The gatekeeper can be an aspect within the unconscious blocking the access point to our repressed emotions. It can block us from finding a deeper repressed emotion that still needs to be accessed.

- Reframing allows us the ability to create a new timeline, changing how past experiences are affecting us today. The reframing process allows us to see things as they are now rather than as who we were when they happened.

- The 3-2-1 process is a model of reframing that creates a new access point to our stories in the past by seeing them from 1st, 2nd, and 3rd person. Feeling our way into these personas helps shift our attachment to these stories.

Shadow Awakening

- The shadow awakening process works for everyone at their own pace. There is no rushing this process, so be patient with your healing.

- Acknowledge the journey you've taken thus far and realize the path is the medicine as we heal our wounds from within.

- The Dark Knight. Make sure to be compassionate as you feel your way into the shadow space. You are working with repressed aspects of yourself that you may not have allowed yourself to feel for years.

- Take note of any areas where you are still projecting your shadow, or where your shadow could still be sabotaging you with old programming. Recognize how you could also be triggering other people's shadow to show up in confrontations.

- Chronic repressed emotions can show up in our bodies and cause dis-ease. Trauma could be running our lives and we become physiologically hard wired or addicted to the hormonal response.

Emotional Mastery

- Emotional Mastery means being tuned into your body, mind, and nervous system. Practice polarizing your emotions so you don't get out of balance when highly triggered.

- Understanding how to polarize your emotions means being aware of the opposing emotion you are feeling and being able to feel your way into the opposing emotion, even when triggered. Instead of feeling fear, you can choose to find faith in a situation.

- Consistently use breathwork in conjunction with your different brainwaves to shift your nervous system, vibrational frequency, and emotions. (This is what we mean by tuning into your body.)

- Get familiar with the five different brainwaves: Beta, Alpha, Theta, Delta, and Gamma. Be aware of which vibrational frequency you are working with to master your nervous system.

- Apply the scale of emotions as a map to measure whether you are in a slow or low vibrational frequency or in a high vibrational frequency. (3D vs. Quantum.)

- Rewire the brain by becoming aware of the meaning you're creating when triggered. Trigger > Meaning > Emotion > Behavior. Get curious about the meaning so you can be conscious of the emotions if you want to change the behavior.

Logical Fallacies

- The word "fallacy," means "false notion or mistaken belief." When we examine language structure, we seek to find logically fallacious arguments hidden within seemingly truthful statements.

- Language arts are like martial arts, and words are like (s)words. Mastering our language structure helps us recognize our inner critic or shadow showing up to sabotage us.

- Eliminate the word "try" from your life. You either do it, or you do not.

- Grammar is assessed through the building blocks of Who, What, When, and Where. This leads to the WHY or Understanding. If we do not understand, it's NOT logical.

- Example fallacies to go over: Red Herring, Ad Hominem, Slippery Slope. Remember, there are hundreds of fallacies to learn.

Boundaries

- Boundaries are what make it possible to ALLOW your dreams to come true. Instead of fighting yourself or your "stories" to stay on track, you just set the parameters and maintain them.

- Boundaries are essential to maintaining your mental, physical, emotional, and spiritual health.

- View your boundaries as a sacred practice. Use your daily rituals as a means of establishing and maintaining your boundaries (both internally and externally).

- Utilize the Law of Gender to recognize where you could be out of balance in your masculine (Yin) or feminine (Yang) energies.

- Being in your masculine or feminine is not "bad" or "good"…but being out of balance in them could show up in pretty ugly ways if we are not aware that these imbalances could be where our shadow is running the show.

Section 2: Shadow Awakening: Course Review

Quantum Thinking

Welcome to the final section of the course work book, please answer these questions below to make sure you understand all the concepts in the course. If you need any support, please contact your course practitioner.

What is the difference between Linear 3D Newtonian thinking and wave-like quantum thinking? (Remember the story of the Chinese farmer.)

_____

_____

_____

_____

How do individuals react from each of the three levels of the brain?

_____

_____

_____

_____

How do you know when you are operating from your highest self?

_____

_____

_____

_____

Shadow Work

What is shadow work?

_____

_____

_____

_____

What are limiting beliefs and the inner critic?

_____

_____

_____

_____

Do you know how to work with your inner child? Are you clear on why it's important to be gentle when accessing it?

_____

_____

_____

_____

Are you clear on what "triggers" are and which ones have been affecting you?

_____

_____

_____

_____

Have you found your "core conflict?" What is it?

_____

_____

_____

_____

Shadow Integration

What is the difference between Shadow work & Shadow integration?

_____

_____

_____

_____

What are the three steps to shadow integration?

_____

_____

_____

_____

Are you clear on what the "gatekeeper" is, and how it blocks you from accessing the shadow?

_____

_____

_____

_____

Do you understand reframing & the 3-2-1 process of reframing trauma? How does it work?

_____

_____

_____

_____

Shadow Awakening

Have you acknowledged your shadow fully and the journey you've taken to access it?

_____

_____

_____

The path is the medicine. Have you opened your heart to access any repressed, suppressed, or denied emotions? How did this impact you?

_____

_____

_____

Have you fully allowed yourself to love your inner child and gently acknowledged its wounds?

_____

_____

_____

Have you taken note of any areas where you could still be projecting your shadow, or where your shadow could still be sabotaging you?

_____

_____

_____

_____

Have you recognized where you could also be triggering other people's shadow to show up? (Even if you are not doing it on purpose.)

_____

_____

_____

_____

Emotional Mastery

Are you aware that trauma and traumatic responses can become physiologically addicting on a hormonal level?

_____

_____

_____

_____

Do you understand how to polarize your emotions to feel an opposing emotion?

_____

_____

_____

_____

Are you aware of how breathwork and meditation can help you shift the function of your brainwaves and change your vibrational frequency?

_____

_____

_____

_____

Can you remember the five different brainwaves?

_____

_____

_____

_____

Are you confident in your ability to identify emotions and the vibrational frequency of those emotions? Low vibes lead to dis-ease.

_____

_____

_____

_____

Are you aware of the meaning you are creating when triggered? What emotions are showing up and which behaviors are consistently occurring based on those emotions?

_____

_____

_____

_____

Logical Fallacies

What does the word "fallacy" mean?

_____

_____

_____

_____

Have you eliminated the word "try" from your life?

_____

_____

_____

_____

What are the 4 building blocks of grammar that create logic, meaning, or why?

_____

_____

_____

_____

Can you name three fallacies? Which ones were the most important to you?

_____

_____

_____

_____

Boundaries

What are boundaries, and why are they so important?

_____

_____

_____

_____

What is the main difference between masculine and feminine energy?

_____

_____

_____

_____

Boundaries are crucial to maintaining your mental and emotional health. Which boundary examples do you remember, and which ones were the most important to you?

_____

_____

_____

_____

Maintaining boundaries helps you live a boundless life. Are you clear on where in your life a lack of boundaries may have sabotaged you or your relationships in the past?

_____

_____

_____

_____

Thank You

Shadow Awakening

Congratulations on completing the Shadow Awakening course and course workbook! We hope you have enjoyed the journey and feel more confident with the vast array of new tools at your disposal to help you navigate your world. Please contact us if you need any more support or have any final questions.

Please connect with me and learn more about my work.

Linktree:
https://linktr.ee/odyandrianos

Website:
Odysseymentorship.com

YouTube:
Odyssey Mentorship

Instagram & TikTok:
iamodywankenobi

Facebook:
Odysseus Andrianos

"The greatest gift you have to give is that of your own self-transformation."

—LAO TZU

BONUS SECTION
The Tao of Shadow Work

The tools we apply to shadow work are quite similar to the ancient wisdom of the *Tao* (usually pronounced "Dow"). When the creation of this workbook and corresponding video course was nearly completed, I discovered deep wisdom within the Taoist philosophy which could be applied in conjunction with this course. In this final bonus chapter of the book, I will share some wisdom of the Tao and how its principles can amplify your skills in both accessing your shadow and awakening your fullest potential as a human being.

The first and most crucial step in understanding the Tao is becoming familiar with the "**Law of Oneness.**" This law describes the connectedness between us, our environment, and our reality. This initial step is highly applicable to shadow work. As we create this awareness of interconnectedness, it becomes easier to see where we may still be projecting our own shadow onto others. This awareness also helps us on the path toward *self-actualization* - where we "actually" achieve our full potential. As we *realize* with our "real eyes" the deep connection we share with our own shadow and everything else around us, we uncover the true GOLD within a deep compassion for ourselves and others.

When we have not integrated our shadow, we will often judge others. In many cases, this judgment of others can act as a mirror into our shadow projections. If our shadow doesn't want us to see something within ourselves, a great way to distract us from it is to project it onto someone else. This lack of self-examination can lead to our suffering. In this space of judgment, we lack compassionate awareness and empathy towards others and ourselves. The greater path is to be a wise observer rather than a judge. Often when we judge, we look down upon others, like a judge sitting above everyone else in the courtroom. And like that judge, we assign blame and label people's actions as "right" or "wrong." When we shift our perspective to become an observer, we can be of greater service because we can see ourselves in others. We come to see each other as "walking together on parallel paths." From this point of view, it is far easier to *walk together* in the space of heartfelt compassion rather than *sitting apart* in a place of judgment.

You may remember in the Shadow Work section of Chapter 2 that we went over how our "positive" traits can often be our shadow hiding right in front of us. This place of judgment can also be where our shadow is hiding our wounds right in front of us. Well, this can also show up with projected "negative" traits as well. This is where practicing compassionate awareness and empathy towards others becomes a mirror into our own lives, allowing us to be gentle observers of ourselves. This objectivity also creates a safe place that's free from judgment where we can become more curious about our emotions and allow space for introspective healing.

At the end of the day, it's all about "energy." Are we using our energy or is it using us? Are we in control of our emotions, or are our emotions controlling us? If we lock away our emotional energy inside of us without compassionate awareness, it can burn us out to where our energy reserves can run dry. Burnout often happens on an unconscious level where we are not even aware we are doing it. After greeting and integrating our own shadow, we can understand where others could be unconsciously projecting their shadow or suppressed emotional energy onto us. Boundaries become super helpful in conserving our energy because we won't be wasting it fighting other peoples' shadows. Navigating projections is where the limbic system could be getting activated or if someone (including ourselves) is consistently highly triggered can become addicted to operating in "fight or flight" mode. The key points to recognize here are that it is all energy. We should be aware of energetic leaks and blockages. Our relationships, including our relationship with ourselves, could be burning our precious life force energy.

Now, speaking of life force energy, let's go a little deeper into the Taoist philosophy and how they interpret energy. This will offer some insight into how you can preserve your precious energy and eliminate energetic leaks.

The 3 Treasures: The 3 Dantians

Let's begin by explaining what a *dantian* is. The dantians are seas of Qi (pronounced "chee"), or energetic centers within the body. The word translates as "*a field of elixir.*" An elixir is a magical or medicinal potion, but in this case the elixir is generated within your own body and can be harnessed to achieve maximal health and performance. The three dantians are **Jing, Qi, and Shen**.

Jing is the foundation of your dantians, and can be compared to the **wax** of a candle also connected to your sacral chakra. The lower dantian is associated with Jing and contains your "**vital essence**," your drive, and your DNA. It is located two to three finger-widths below your navel in the middle of your abdomen, at your center of gravity. This is where we get "gut feelings" about things. It could also be described as your sexual energy where your Yin & Yang energies combine as the foundation of your energetic field.

Qi is the energy that emanates from all life and is known as your "**life force.**" It can be compared to the **flame** of a candle, also relating to your heart chakra. The middle dantian is associated with Qi which is the emotional center of the body. Many people have heard of Qi in the West, but most people have not been instructed in how to use Qi to cultivate Jing. This is a great example of where emotional energy that is held within the body can create "energetic blocks," which can manifest as disease within the body. We'll get into this more later.

Shen is the "**spirit**" which dwells within the body and is also called the "third eye." It can be compared to the **light** emanating from a candle. The upper dantian is associated with Shen and is considered the spiritual element of a person's psyche. Shen relates to shadow work as when we experience emotional pain, it can fragment our psyche, creating dissociation and dysfunction related to unconscious self-sabotage from the shadow realm.

A great way to remember the *dantians* is to combine the three elements to get the complete candle - the Jing is the wax, the Qi is the flame, and the Shen is the light emanating from the flame. This image can help us visualize how we could be "burning out" our energy. When we eat poorly, drink too much alcohol, or abuse drugs, this can create an unstable flame (Qi). An unstable flame may melt the wax (Jing) unevenly and allow the candle to burn too quickly or sideways. This also makes the light of the (Shen) go dim so we cannot see our shadow around the light becoming stronger. People can also get sick because they are misusing their Qi and burning up their Jing. We only have a limited amount of Jing in this life, and when it runs out… we die. This is why it's so important to cultivate our Qi life force energy.

What we take into our bodies is crucial to our performance - mentally, physically, emotionally, and spiritually. Qi emanates and runs throughout the organs of the body. The food that we eat is processed and turned into Qi. The air that we breathe is transformed and combined with our food to cultivate Qi within the body. It's the same with the water that we drink it's all Qi energy. This is why it's so important to get high quality food, water, and oxygen to aid your peak performance.

When we get stuck in deep emotional pain, when we're not breathing properly or moving our bodies, when we're not eating healthy...our Qi energy (life force) begins to slowly grow weaker. Imagine the candle flame getting dimmer. When this happens, the light from the candle also grows dimmer. This creates opportunities for the shadow to start running the show, and is a massive problem facing society today. An example of this could be a friend or family member who experienced a serious addiction to drugs or alcohol. Because of the massive blockages of Qi in their bodies, they lost control of themselves. This is what we mean by our shadow running our lives. The drugs, alcohol, or poor diet can be a physical manifestation of feeding those repressed or suppressed emotions because the deeper internal emotional dis-ease has not been addressed.

I personally appreciate how this ancient Taoist philosophy explains the flow (or blockage) of energy within the body through the perspective of the three dantians. After explaining this concept to others, I've even had clients text me and say how they were conserving their Jing or that someone was trying to steal their Jing and it helped them center themselves and prevent "energetic leaks" in their day-to-day life.

Let's go a little deeper into how our energetic leaks relate to the Tao, and how many people are unbalanced in today's society. Possibly one of the most widely recognized symbols in the world is the Yin & Yang. This symbol can represent many things, but the foundational point is that the Yang is *masculine* and the Yin is *feminine*. We touched on this briefly in the boundaries section of Chapter 6 and should mention it again because it is crucial to understand how your energy is expressed. Are you deeply entrenched in your yin feminine energy, or are you constantly externally oriented in your Yang masculine energy? The truth is that most people are burning themselves out by staying in their masculine Yang energy.

We can think of Yang energy expressed by a male peacock showing off its tail feathers to attract a mate. Much of modern society lives like this, with everyone showing off and constantly seeking external attention. These actions create a great spiritual poverty for humanity because we live so out of balance with our Yin energies. Yin is the receptive state of resting, calming down, and healing our bodies. In Chapter 1 we went over the *3D vs. quantum* models of thinking. This is another expression of the masculine and feminine nature of humanity. So many of us are locked into the masculine, linear, Yang energy that we cannot even see our shadow. This lack of internal introspection is at the root of so much mental and emotional disease within society. When we take the time to investigate our internal world from the feminine Yin perspective, it allows us the time and space to heal. This also helps us to eliminate energetic leaks as we acknowledge our shadow and heal our emotional pain.

One powerful tool we can use to shift our internal emotional energy is breathwork. Utilize the recordings included with this book to activate your parasympathetic nervous system and help you get out of your head space and become more grounded in your body. This pairs perfectly with Taoist philosophy as breathwork is a great way to strengthen and steady our Qi (flame). It also helps us to work out any energetic blocks or leakages that are burning through our Jing (wax). (*Remember the candle analogy.*)

By applying breathwork and meditation, we begin to calm the nervous system. Once the nervous system is calm, we can then begin to fall into rest and recovery mode, where the process of deeper healing begins. The parasympathetic nervous system is also where we can rest deeply in our divine feminine (Yin) nature, get out of our heads, and connect with our hearts. In this space we can stop running away from our emotions by keeping our minds constantly busy. We can finally bring our emotions to the surface in this restful space, and can begin to process them and start our deeper healing. This process brings awareness to any blocks or leaks where emotional energy is not circulating properly, and helps clear these energetic blocks where our Qi could be causing physical discomfort and burning through our Jing.

One of my favorite quotes about emotional mastery and how it relates to Taoist philosophy comes from Lillian Bridges, an expert in Taoist healing and specifically Chinese face reading. She said, *"There is no such thing as a good or bad emotion, only stuck emotions."* This quote hits the nail on the head. Our emotions are our teachers, but we can't learn what they are trying to teach us if we keep them hidden away in the shadows. This is what creates stuck Qi energy, but the great news is that we can transmute that energy and harness it. We can actually access stored or dormant Jing energy and use it to live a more fulfilling life.

Taoist healing wisdom is a VERY deep subject. We are only touching on some of the basics related to shadow work. The key point is that emotions are energy and could be seen as our Qi or "life force" energy. This is not recognized by most Western medicine which is astounding but has been known for thousands of years in Eastern medicine. I would like to mention that I don't believe that either Western or Eastern medicine is better or worse. Both should be utilized harmoniously in the healing process. Western medicine often takes a more masculine (yang) approach, whereas eastern healing modalities are generally more feminine (yin). The imbalances we face in our Western medicine paradigm are that, in many cases we use drugs to numb our emotions instead of facing them, which keeps us from doing the actual work to heal our internal pain. A blend of both Western and Eastern modalities provides greater potential for long-term healing. In some cases, drugs are an excellent option, but they can be like a crutch that can turn into a handicap if used for too long.

One of my favorite explanations of the shortcomings of using only Western medicine alone is from Dr. Thurman Fleet, who explained that much of Western medicine fails to address the root causes of our health problems and only deals with the effects. So many people develop mental health problems because the root cause is not addressed. The physical problem that the doctors see and are trying to treat does not actually get healed because they're attempting to treat the physical effects instead of getting to the energetic root cause. Not addressing the root cause which in many cases is emotional pain begins to turn into a mental health problem because all the treatments only work on the physical body. The deeper emotional issue is not being addressed, and the symptoms which are signals to dive deeper are masked and suppressed with drugs. The root cause of the physical pain is the emotional pain that is often not even acknowledged. Not only does the patient not heal, they begin to develop mental health problems as a result.

I am not a doctor, but I wonder if diseases for which doctors do not know the cause might be related to suppressed, repressed, denied, or masked emotions. Fibromyalgia, rheumatoid arthritis, lupus, and certain types of cancer...there is no consensus among doctors about what causes these diseases. Here is where I ask the question: "Could it be our dormant emotional pain (or stuck Qi energy) manifesting as dis-ease within the body?" Perhaps we could learn to heal our stuck emotional energy to release our Jing so we can heal and live a more fulfilling life. I'm not a doctor, but I do have a degree in kinesiology. Over my 20 years of coaching, I've seen how certain clients' bodies struggled to move efficiently and upon further inquiry found out they were often holding on to emotional pain.

I often mention to my clients that the future of health, healing, and medicine lies in healing our emotional pain and learning to calm down our nervous system. These two components go hand in hand. As we heal our emotional pain and learn to calm down our nervous system, our calm nervous system allows us to better access our emotional pain. This acts as a positive feedback loop, building momentum to move from our energy being stuck to transmuting that energy for future use. The unblocked Qi (*energy*) allows us to fully access our Jing (*vital essence*) and connect with our Shen (*spirit*). This connection won't be taught in Western medicine anytime soon, but it has been known in ancient Taoist philosophy for ages. At the foundational level, the greatest healing occurs when we reconnect with our souls and are grounded in our physical bodies. When the three *dantians* are working harmoniously, we can rest assured that our bodies will perform at an optimal level. The chances of disease will be diminished when our nervous system is calm and we are no longer suppressing our emotional energy.

Shadow work at its roots is essentially Taoism *applied*. When we've stopped living our lives in a constant Yang (masculine) energetic state, and we've acknowledged our dark (Yin) energy, we can live a more balanced and harmonious life "in tune" with our inner nature. This is also known as "The Middle Way Path." By balancing our Yin and Yang energies, we move through life with greater ease because we've faced and integrated our emotional wounds which leads to less energetic leaks, and more compassion for ourselves, others, and the world. This compassion and loving awareness are the attunement we are all unconsciously seeking. Instead of looking for it outside of ourselves, we can become aware that it was always already within us. We can flow effortlessly in a *quantum* state of mind, and create the life of our dreams, because we are worth it and we deserve it!

I hope this book has inspired you, challenged you to grow, and helped you look at your life in new ways. Please reach out with any questions or comments. I appreciate you for engaging in this work. I want to finish by mentioning that, as you acknowledge your emotional pain and begin healing your shadow, this also heals humanity's collective shadow. I am grateful you have taken the time to embark on this journey. Thank you.

"The shadow is needed now more than ever. We heal the world when we heal ourselves, and hope shines brightest when it illuminates the dark."

- Sasha Graham

RESOURCES

Referenced Books &
Recommended Reading

Becoming Supernatural, Dr. Joe Dispenza

Rays of Dawn, Dr. Thurman Fleet

Gold Mining The Shadows, Pixie Lighthorse

Boundaries & Protection, Pixie Lighthorse

The Body Keeps The Score, Bessel Van Kolk

Fasting The Mind, Jason Gregory

Bringing Your Shadow out of the Dark, Robert Augustus Masters

Face Reading in Chinese Medicine, Lillian Bridges

The Tibetan Book of Living & Dying, Sogyal Rinpoche

Wetiko, Paul Levy

The Tao of Chaos, Stephen Wolinsky

Courses & Community Support

Awaken Your Inner Author, www.awakenyourinnerauthor.com

Download Melissa's Magic system to *finally* write the book that's trapped in your mind and heart.

As aspiring authors, we dream of our book creating a movement for the world and financial freedom for ourselves. But far too often, what happens instead is the soul-crushing experience of publishing your book only to have sales fall flat, momentum stunted, and your potentially life-changing book reaches precious few people. We are dedicated to making sure your story ends quite differently -- with you creating the impact and income that you desire from your book. That's where the publishing partnership with Ultimate Vida comes in. Grounded with decades of experience in online marketing and building sound business models around books, we help authors sidestep land- mines and reach their goals by providing actionable data (like title and cover testing), a deep and intimate understanding of who your audience actually is (which is bound to surprise you), strategic advice on offerings beyond the book, and ongoing monthly income opportunities that far exceed book royalties. Reach out to melissa@uncorpedinfluence.com to discuss strategies to make a splash with your book and incorporate the Ultimate Vida community experience and course as a new revenue stream.

.

Join the Ultimate Vida Freedom Circle

Your Secret Weapon To Kiss Your Job Goodbye in as Little as 77 Days, Build an Online Tribe, and Leave a Legacy

As an Ultimate Vida Freedom Circle Member, you can:

- Create a baseline of time and financial freedom while doing work you love

- Access proprietary data and strategies to blissfully use your newly integrated shadow as a guide in your entrepreneurial journey

- Get FREE access to our flagship Freedom Blueprint course, which sells on its own for $1,500

- Use your newfound freedom to focus on health, wellness, relationships, and purpose...the things that make life worth living

- Connect with the world's most epic tribe of freedom seekers to enrich your life, help you achieve your goals, and form lifelong friendships

- Earn supplemental income or even life-changing monthly money by referring others into the community

Enjoy the Community for FREE for 14 days!
www.ultimatevida.com/awakening

ABOUT THE AUTHOR

Odysseus Andrianos

www.odysseymentorship.com

Odysseus Andrianos has a degree in Kinesiology from San Diego State University as well as multiple coaching certifications. He has been a lifestyle and wellness coach for over 20 years accumulating over 20,000 hours of experience. He built his first coaching facility when he was 24 years old which he ran for 11 years. Eventually he opened a second coaching facility with the largest female-owned corporation in the San Francisco Bay Area.

Early in his career, Odysseus realized that exercise and diet alone weren't enough to give people the lasting results they deserve. He discovered something magical as he delved deeper into psychology, quantum physics, and ancient eastern philosophy: the missing link to not only sustained results, but the keys to living a deeply fulfilling life lies in our ability to access, work with, and heal through our emotions. He believes the future of health, fitness, medicine, and healing comes down to emotions, the nervous system, and quantum psychology. This book is a culmination of all of his years of coaching to develop a do-it-yourself approach to work with your emotions and setting yourself free from your inner emotional pain. Learn more and contact Odysseus at www.odysseymentorship.com

Made in the USA
Middletown, DE
03 August 2022